Sunderland

KEY
Books

HISTORIC MILITARY AIRCRAFT SERIES, VOLUME 23

Contents page image: A Short Brothers Sunderland in flight.

Published by Key Books
An imprint of Key Publishing Ltd
PO Box 100
Stamford
Lincs PE9 1XQ

www.keypublishing.com

Original edition published as *Aeroplane Icons: Sunderland*
© 2012, edited by Martyn Chorlton

This edition © 2022

ISBN 978 1 80282 458 2

Typeset by SJmagic DESIGN SERVICES, India.

Contents

The Queen of the Flying Boats

T he arrival of the Short Sunderland in RAF service in 1938 raised the bar considerably with regard to flying boat design, compared to what airmen had previously experienced. Gone were the draughty, cluttered cockpits, cramped fuselages and mediocre performance associated with average inter-war flying boats. The Sunderland brought a host of improvements, which remained, only marginally altered, for the aircraft's 21 years of RAF service. Those crews still operating the Saro London and Supermarine Stranraer must have looked on in envy as the Sunderland crews enjoyed a 'bridge', a galley, a dining room and even a sleeping area, thanks to the flying boat's cavernous hull.

Coastal Command would operate almost 50 different types during World War Two, but only the Sunderland would continually serve on the front line from the first day to the last. This, and the fact that the flying boat remained in RAF service until 1958 – and almost a decade beyond with the RNZAF – is testimony to the aircraft's forward-thinking design.

The Sunderland was by far the best flying boat the RAF had ever received and, sadly, was also the last. It reluctantly gave way to another RAF stalwart, the Avro Shackleton, when military policy dictated that maritime operations could more efficiently be carried out by land-based aircraft. The last three remaining Sunderlands were withdrawn from service in 1960, with ML824 making a nostalgic final flight to Pembroke Dock in 1961.

The Sunderland holds a very special place in virtually every aviation enthusiast's heart, and even more so to the thousands of aircrews who served on one of the RAF's 'Queen of Boats'. It was a unique experience, the combination of water, aircraft and large tight-knit crew working together for hours on end. During the post-war period, those lucky enough to still be serving with the type were branded part of the 'Flying Boat Union', such was the feeling of camaraderie and specialism that was experienced by all who worked on, or flew, the big flying boat.

Mk I L2160, the third production Sunderland, photographed only days before it joined 209 Squadron on 18 May 1939. (*Aeroplane*)

Chapter 1

The Sunderland Story

Genesis

Our journey begins in 1908, when three brothers, Horace Leonard, Albert Eustace and Hugh Oswald Short, each invested £200 to form Short Brothers. The sole purpose of this new company was to design and build aircraft, effectively making Short Brothers the world's first commercial aircraft manufacturing business.

Prior to the brothers' groundbreaking enterprise, both Horace and Oswald had made their first flights in balloons in 1897. At the same time, the duo began manufacturing balloons on a site beneath the arches at the LBSC (London, Brighton and South Coast) Railway, Battersea Park in London. They were quickly steered away from balloons when they heard that the Wright Brothers were carrying out a series of demonstration flights across France in 1908. Eustace and Oswald both attended at least one demonstration flight and, without Horace even setting his eyes on one of the Wright's aircraft, persuaded Horace to create Short Brothers. By February the following year, Eustace had obtained a licence to build six Wright Flyers, all of which would be sold to the fledgling Aero Club (later the Royal Aero Club). A single glider for the use of the Hon. Charles S. Rolls and a privately designed aircraft for Frank McClean, were also contracted to be built by the new company.

In March 1909, the Short Brothers' very first 'factory' was constructed on land near Leysdown, Isle of Sheppey, Kent, comprising a single corrugated iron shed measuring 100ft by 45ft. By the summer, a second shed of similar size was erected and the world's first aircraft production contract for the six Wright Flyers was completed in February 1910. While work was progressing, Horace had been designing the company's first aircraft, called the Short Biplane No. 1. Admittedly, the aircraft bore

A lone Sunderland captured in its natural environment en route to its patrol area in the North Atlantic! (*Aeroplane*)

There is no doubting the influence of the Wright Brothers on the Short Brothers' early aircraft. This is the Short No. 3 (Model A) flying from Eastchurch in 1910. (Via Martyn Chorlton)

a strong resemblance to the Flyer, but this aircraft, built for Frank McClean, was the first of many designed and built solely by the company.

In April 1910, the Short factory was moved to Eastchurch, with more space to expand and a good sized landing ground located close by. It was here that the first four Royal Navy officers began their pilot training with Short Brothers, including Lt Charles Rumney Samson and Lt Arthur Longmore, both of whom were enthusiastic about the aircraft's potential as a useful tool for the navy.

In 1913, the company had to build a second factory for seaplane production on the banks of the River Medway at Rochester. By the beginning of World War One, the demand for Short Brothers aircraft was so high that the company could not cope single-handedly. To deal with this, the Admiralty issued a host of licences to subcontractors, many of whom went on to become great aircraft manufacturers in their own right. Tractor floatplanes, such as the world's first torpedo bomber, the Short Type 184, were in particularly high demand and Short Brothers, which already had a full order book, was also commissioned to build a pair of rigid airships, No. 31 and No. 32. To fulfil the contract, land was purchased at Cardington, near Bedford, where a giant airship shed was constructed. While the shed was being erected, contracts were also received to build the R.37 and R.38 but, by 1919, the whole Cardington site was nationalised to become the Royal Airship Works. Duly compensated, Short Brothers withdrew from airship construction, but still contributed a whole design team to help in the completion of the R.38.

And then there were two

It was on 6 April 1917 that the eldest brother, Horace, passed away at Eastchurch following a short illness. Eustace was still looking after the Battersea balloon factory, which left the Rochester factory to Oswald to supervise. By now, Rochester had become the main headquarters for Short Brothers, while the Eastchurch works was transferred to the Royal Navy Air Service (RNAS).

Prior to Horace's passing, the brothers were unable to pursue the idea of designing and developing their own flying boats because of their older sibling's refusal to take part in the notion. However, with Horace's death, Oswald wasted no time accepting Admiralty contracts for Felixstowe F.3s and F.5s to be built at Rochester for the RNAS. By 1918, Short Brothers submitted its own tender for a twin-engined biplane flying boat called the N.3 Cromarty. Three prototypes were ordered, but following the Armistice in 1918, the order was reduced to a single aircraft. The sole Cromarty, N120, first flew on 19 April 1921 and, following a host of modifications, was accepted by the RAF. Its career was short though, as it was damaged on landing in St Mary's Roads, Scilly Islands, in August 1922 and was reduced to scrap in situ. No further orders for the Cromarty were forthcoming, but the experience gained from building the F.3s and F.5s gave Oswald and his team the experience they needed to continue designing and building flying boats.

When World War One came to end, despite the company's successes and achievements in such a short space of time, Short Brothers was not immune to the sudden downward demand for aircraft. The company, like so many others, had to diversify or die. During the early 1920s, Short manufactured barges, lifeboats and motorboats and, in 1924, also began production of lightweight bodies for London omnibuses.

Oswald's thinking was still firmly entrenched in building aircraft and his foresight in design was put to the test in 1916, when he produced the first metal airframe components made of duralumin. Oswald was rightly convinced that metal would replace wood, particularly in flying boats, where water-soaked hulls on the Felixstowes severely inhibited performance. Oswald's views on the subject were not shared by many at the time and, determined to prove the point, he proceeded with a private venture to build an all-metal single-seat biplane. Initially named the Swallow, by the time the aircraft was on display at the Olympia Aero Show on 9 July 1920, it had been renamed the 'Silver Streak'. The airframe contained no wood whatsoever, just various steels, aluminium skin and duralumin. The mistrust of such a design was probably the reason why a Certificate of Airworthiness was not issued, but the Air Ministry, on the other hand, was intrigued by the 'Silver Streak'. The RAF modified the aircraft as a two-seater and spent the next two years putting the 'Silver Streak' through a host of tests and trials in an attempt to justify all the scepticism over all-metal designs. While very little was officially said about the aircraft, it appears that the testing had shown that all-metal designs worked and a military version of the 'Silver Streak' – the S.3 Springbok – was contracted in 1922, with a view to replacing the RAF's ageing F.2Bs and DH.9As. However, prejudice against metal aircraft lingered on, and only five Springboks were built, none of them serving with the RAF.

The one and only Short N.3 Cromarty N120 taxiing on the River Medway in late 1921. The aircraft would prove to be a very influential design for future Short Brothers flying boat projects. (Via Martyn Chorlton)

The military version of the 'Silver Streak' was the all-metal S.3 Springbok, of which only five were built, but once again the experience and data gained would stand the company's design teams in good stead. (Via Martyn Chorlton)

Left: The Short S.5 Singapore Mk I N179. Despite being the better performer, a full production contract was awarded to Blackburn. (Via Martyn Chorlton)

Below: Named *City of Alexandria* by Imperial Airways, S.8 Calcutta G-EBVG served with the airline until 28 December 1936, when the aircraft capsized in a storm at Mirabella, Crete. (Via Martyn Chorlton)

The metal-hulled flying boat arrives

By 1924, the Air Ministry invited aircraft manufacturers to tender a 'modern design' to replace the wooden hulls of its Felixstowe F.5s, which were still in operational service. There was clearly no mention of metal, but, even though officialdom got in the way, this did not stop Oswald from gaining a contract to design and build a single metal hull. This was to be fitted to F.5 N177 and, in its hybrid guise, the flying boat first flew from the River Medway on 5 January 1925. By March, N177 was in the hands of the Marine Aircraft Experimental Establishment (MAEE) at Felixstowe, which called the flying boat the 'Tin Five'. The F.5 performed well with its new lightweight metal hull, and as a result, Oswald was finally vindicated, and an order for an all-metal version of the original Cromarty was placed. Under Specification 13/24 the result was the Singapore Mk I, N179, which first flew on 17 August 1926. The Singapore performed head and shoulders above its rivals at Blackburn, Saunders and Supermarine. However, the production order was issued to Blackburn and the lone Singapore was transferred to the MAEE. N179 was later loaned back to Short, which prepared the flying boat for British aviation pioneer Sir Alan Cobham to fly a 23,000-mile-long survey of Africa for Imperial Airways. Re-registered as G-EBUP, the Singapore successfully completed the task and, in June 1929, the stalwart aircraft was back with the Air Ministry.

The design of the Singapore laid the foundation blocks for the Calcutta, which was primarily designed for Imperial Airways. The airline initially ordered two aircraft, G-EBVG and G-EBVH, which made their first flights on 14 February and 3 May 1928, respectively. In the end, only five Calcuttas were built for Imperial Airways, although two others were sold in France and six more were modified extensively for the RAF as Rangoons. The first three, S1433, S1434 and S1345, were flown to Basra in 1931 for 203 Squadron, to replace its Supermarine Southampton Mk II. K2134, K2809 and K3678 followed in 1934. By August/September 1935, all six Rangoons were on their way back to the UK, where five of them were transferred to 210 Squadron at Pembroke Dock.

In the meantime, the Short Brothers design team was working flat out to develop the original Singapore into a four-engined fully militarised aircraft. Reluctantly, Short Brothers was given a contract to build a single prototype, known as the Singapore Mk II, and N246 first flew on 27 March 1930. Service trials followed with the MAEE and a short list of modifications were suggested, including changing the flying boat's large single fin and rudder to a triple-fin arrangement that could incorporate a rear gunner's position. Following successful trials in August 1933, a production order for just four aircraft was placed for the renamed Singapore Mk III. The first aircraft, K3592, flew on 15 June 1934, and, following further production orders, the type first entered service with 203 Squadron at Basra to replace the unit's Rangoons. 205, 209, 210, 228, 230 and 240 squadrons went on to operate the Singapore Mk III, despite only 37 eventually being built. Many went on to serve on the front line until 1941, and four examples had extended service with 5 Squadron Royal New Zealand Air Force (RNZAF) at Fiji until 1945.

The 'Tin Five' Felixstowe F.5 N177, with its revolutionary all-metal hull, makes a low pass over the Medway in late 1925. (Via Martyn Chorlton)

Above: The first of three S.8 Rangoons delivered to 203 Squadron was S1433 in 1931, one of only six built, which served until 1936. (Via Martyn Chorlton)

Left: Singapore Mk II N246 seen in its original form with the large single fin, which was later replaced by a triple-fin layout, incorporating a rear gunner's position. (Via Martyn Chorlton)

And then there was one

It was a regular custom for Eustace Short to fly to work and, on 8 April 1932, his Mussel Mk II amphibian landed perfectly, as usual, on the River Medway. However, rather than taxiing to its usual mooring, the aircraft drifted on, as lifeless as its occupant. Eustace was found dead in the cockpit, having suffered a heart attack.

At the time of his death, the company was going through a vibrant period of experimentation; innovations including the incredible Sarafand flying boat. The six-engined aircraft had a wingspan of 120ft, was nearly 90ft long and, in the capable hands of the company's chief test pilot, John Parker, had made a tentative ten-minute maiden flight on 30 June 1932. Basically a scaled up version of the Singapore Mk II, the Sarafand was the world's second largest aircraft at the time. Serialled S1589, the giant flying boat was designed with a ten-man crew in mind and was accepted by the RAF for trials.

JOHN LANKESTER PARKER OBE, FRAES HON., MSLAE (1896 TO 22 AUGUST 1965)

Parker joined Short Brothers in 1916 as a part-time test pilot and assistant to the company's chief test pilot, Ronald Kemp. Parker cut his flying teeth working for the Northern Aircraft Company at Windermere from 1914 to 1916. During his time in Cumbria, Parker met Capt (later Adm Sir) Murray Sueter, Kemp and Oscar Gnosspelius, all of whom would become influential in his career.

He first worked for Short Brothers on 17 October 1916, when he was asked by Horace Short to test fly six Short bombers from Eastchurch. His flying skills impressed and, by 1918, he had already taken over from Kemp as chief test pilot. From 1918 to his last flight as chief test pilot on 22 August 1945, Parker flew every Short prototype built during that period on their maiden flights. This colossal range of types spread from the Shirl to the Shetland.

After achieving an excellent record of performance that outclassed all contemporary designs, the Sarafand was eventually scrapped at Felixstowe in 1936.

Another good example of all-metal construction at work was the R.24/31 Knuckleduster. A novel gull-wing, twin-engined monoplane, Knuckleduster K3574 first flew on 30 November 1933. Although it was another opportunity for Oswald to push his all-metal designs a little further, the primary function of the Knuckleduster was to test the steam-cooled Rolls-Royce Goshawk engines. During trials, the engines and airframe were constantly modified before the aircraft was retired in 1938, as an instructional airframe at Cosford. Regardless, the Knuckleduster had provided Short Brothers with a great deal of information that would prove invaluable to the company in the years ahead.

Imperial Empire

The 1930s, with regard to the civilian market for Short Brothers, continued to see a demand for flying boats from Imperial Airways. In response, a larger, four-engined version of the Calcutta was built, now known as the Kent. Just three Kents were built, all ordered for Imperial Airways and registered as G-ABFA *Scipio*, G-ABFB *Syvanus* and G-ABFC *Satyrus*, respectively. All were employed on the airline's overseas routes; G-ABFA first flying on 24 February 1931. All gave good service through the mid- to late-1930s; the last, G-ABFC, continued to serve until it was scrapped at Hythe in 1938. Imperial Airways also ordered two land plane versions of the Kent, the S.17/L, registered as G-ACJJ *Scylla* and G-ACJK *Syrinx*. Both remained in service with Imperial Airways right up to the beginning of World War Two and enjoyed brief service with the RAF, becoming the last Short Brothers biplane designs still in use.

When the Imperial Airways proposal for the Empire Air Mail Scheme was approved by the government in December 1934, Short Brothers could not have known how significant this decision would be to the company. At a similar time, Imperial Airways also made the decision to re-equip all of its trunk routes with flying boats in order to increase the efficiency of passenger, mail and freight transfers between aircraft. As a result, Imperial Airways asked Short Brothers to submit proposals for a much-improved version of the Kent, which could transport 24 passengers and up to 1½ tons of mail over a range of 800 miles. The design team, led by Arthur Gouge, initially considered another biplane layout. Wisely, the team produced a clean looking, four-engined monoplane that was designated the S.23. Imperial Airways only requested a pair of prototypes at first, but when the design was shown to the airline, it discarded the idea of the two prototypes and went for a full production order of 14 aircraft, which later increased to 28. Imperial Airways referred to its latest Short Brothers acquisition as the C-Class, but these were soon referred to worldwide as the Empire Boats. The first and flagship C-Class flying boat was G-ADHL *Canopus*, which first flew from the River Medway on 3 July 1936, with G-ADHM *Caledonia* following on 11 September. An order for three more C-Class flying boats was also placed by QANTAS (Queensland and Northern Territory Aerial Services) not long after full production of the type began; a further dozen modified versions, designated the S.30 and S.33, were also built. The Empire Boats certainly raised the bar for long distance passenger comfort and improved the efficiency of mail delivery, right up to the beginning of the war. During World War Two, many continued to serve as civilian airliners and RAF transport aircraft until 1945.

The gigantic Short Sarafand was one of the world's largest aircraft when it first flew in June 1932. (Via Martyn Chorlton)

The unique and novel Knuckleduster provided Short Brothers with a large amount of data that would ultimately benefit the design of the Sunderland. (Via Martyn Chorlton)

A four-engined version of the Calcutta, three Kents were built, all for Imperial Airways in 1931. G-ABFA *Scipio*, the first of the three, is pictured on the Medway. The aircraft sank off Crete on 22 August 1936. (Via Martyn Chorlton)

Bigger and better?

A scaled-up version of the S.23 was also developed by Short and this flying boat would represent the biggest it had produced so far, even larger than the Sarafand. The S.26 had a wingspan of 134ft 4in and a fuselage 101ft 4in long. The flying boat was designed for direct transatlantic mail services and the first of just three, later designated as the G-Class boat, G-AFCI *Golden Hind* first flew on 21 July 1939. G-AFCJ *Grenadier* and G-AFCK *Grenville* followed, but by September 1939, all three had been requisitioned by the RAF. By this time, two of them had been renamed: *Grenadier* was renamed *Golden Fleece* and *Grenville* was re-titled *Golden Horn*. The RAF wasted no time pressing the giant flying boats into military service, being quite desperate to have as many long-range aircraft operating for Coastal Command as possible. All were modified by Short Brothers to become the S.26/M and were delivered to the RAF as X8275, X8274 and X8273, respectively. Military conversion included the fitment of a pair of dorsal turrets and a Boulton Paul BPA Mk II rear turret; all S.26/Ms were fitted with four .303in machine guns. Racks for eight 500lb bombs were fitted under the wings and, internally, the G-Class carried 28 flame floats, 20 reconnaissance flares and eight smoke floats. Air to Surface Vessel (ASV) radar technology was fitted and the fuel tanks and crew positions were protected by armour plating. Airborne Surveillance Radar (ASR) was also retrofitted to all three aircraft by Blackburn Aircraft Ltd at Dumbarton. The big flying boats all saw service with 10 Squadron, the RAAF and 119 Squadron, and the surviving two continued to serve with British Overseas Aircraft Corporation (BOAC), following reconversion to a passenger layout. X8274 *Golden Fleece* was lost en route to Gibraltar on 21 June 1941, after the flying boat ditched off Cape Finisterre and sank. Nine airmen lost their lives, while another five survived to become prisoners of war (POWs). *Golden Horn* was also wrecked in a crash at Lisbon on 9 January 1943. *Golden Hind* survived to make its last flight on 17 April 1948 and was scrapped in 1954.

Short Brothers' final large flying boat design, which was intended to be a replacement for the Sunderland in RAF service, was the huge S.35 Shetland. Work began in 1944 on two prototypes, each with a wingspan of 150ft 4in. The first, DX166, flew for the first time on 14 December 1944. DX166 was later destroyed by fire while moored at MAEE, Felixstowe, on 28 January 1948, although by now, a second aircraft, Shetland Mk II DX171 was carrying out trials of its own. The military serial was never actually painted onto the flying boat and the aircraft was actually registered as G-AGVD, first flying on

17 September 1947. The Shetland was trialled by BOAC but was destined never to carry a fare-paying passenger before it was scrapped in 1951. Several proposed developments of the Shetland remained firmly on the drawing board, with it becoming apparent that the age of the flying boat was, sadly, well and truly over.

Short's final flying boat design was the SA.6 Sealand, a small twin-engined amphibian designed for commercial feeder operations. Drawing from decades of experience, the Sealand was of sound design but only 25 were built. The Sealand first flew on 22 January 1948, bringing to an end Short Brothers' 40-year association with flying boat aircraft designs. The company had also designed some excellent land-based aircraft, including the Stirling and, later, the Belfast and Skyvan, but Short Brothers would always primarily be associated with the flying boat. Not only that, the first name that many would associate with the Kent-based company, would emphatically be the Sunderland.

The first S.23 C-Class flying boat, G-ADHL, thereafter known as Empire Boat, set new standards in international air travel and passenger comfort. *Canopus* gave good service with Imperial Airways and, later, British Overseas Aircraft Corporation (BOAC) during World War Two, before being broken up at Hythe in November 1946. (Via Martyn Chorlton)

One of the three S.26 G-Class flying boats requisitioned by the RAF in September 1939. Ex-G-AFCJ was serialled X8274 and, as can been seen here, is looking very warlike in camouflage with a formidable defensive armament of 12 .303 in machine guns in three turrets. (Via Martyn Chorlton)

Shetland Mk I DX166 cruising over St Mary's Marshes, Hoo Peninsula, heading towards Canvey Island. (Charles E. Brown)

The last flying boat produced by Short Brothers was the SA.6 Sealand. Like the Shetland before it, times had moved on and, despite Britain being an island nation, there was no demand for this type of aircraft anymore. (Via Martyn Chorlton)

The Sunderland

Only weeks before the design team began working on the S.23 Empire Boat, production of the S.25 Sunderland had also commenced. This often leads to some confusion and the incorrect statement that the S.25 was the military derivative of the S.23. The Sunderland project came about because of an Air Ministry invitation to tender a four-engined, long-range flying boat for the RAF to meet Specification R.2/33, issued on 23 September 1933. Not long after this specification was issued, Imperial Airways made a request for a separate design, which would become the S.23.

R.2/33 listed several general requirements, the most significant being the ability to achieve a range of 1,400 sea miles at 2,000ft, at normal cruising speed, with a full reconnaissance load. Landing speed should not be higher than 55kts, service ceiling no less than 15,000ft and the aircraft should be able to continue to fly on two engines with a full military load and three engines with a maximum load. The crew was planned to total six, including two pilots, with sleeping accommodation for all, as well as full catering/galley for long-range operations. Armament requirement was to include four air gunners' positions, each with a single .303 in Lewis machine gun with necessary mountings. Another defensive option was the incorporation of a 37mm COW cannon in the bow of the flying boat, while one more suggestion was the fitment of two COW cannons in a vertical fixed position, firing downwards through a planning bottom, with watertight mountings. Common sense prevailed and both COW cannon ideas were dropped in favour of a single .303 in Lewis or Vickers 'K' machine gun in a Frazer-Nash FN11 gun turret mounted in the nose. Rear defence was to be provided by an FN13 turret mounting four .303 in machine guns.

The FN13 turret was quite a heavy piece of equipment, and the result was a shift in the centre of gravity. To compensate, the original wing design, which was straight, had to be swept back by 4¼°, and the main step under the hull had to be moved rearwards a corresponding distance, which in turn changed the step depth. The modified sweepback left all four engines at a slight angle to the path of flight. All these modifications were formalised for the pending production aircraft but the prototype S.25 Sunderland, K4774, would remain straight winged during its very early flights.

The original requests issued by the Air Ministry and Imperial Airways for the S.25 Sunderland and the S.23 Empire Boat made no indication as to the wing layout and both could have become biplanes. However, it was while Oswald Short, Arthur Gouge and John Parker were perusing aircraft lined up for the start of the MacRobertson Air Race at Mildenhall in October 1934, that inspiration was drawn from one of the entrants. The Douglas DC-2 monoplane airliner impressed all who laid eyes upon it; its appearance alone was advanced, not to mention the modern equipment on board and its carrying capability. On the Short team's return to Rochester, a monoplane design was confirmed for both flying boats, and an older company design, the Scion Senior, was used as a template. The Scion was a good performer and the general layout and geometry of its design, plus the fact that its Pobjoy Niagara engines were half the size of the proposed Pegasus planned for the S.25, led the design team to simply double the dimensions as a starting point for the new flying boats. The Scion Senior continued to play an important role in the design process of both flying boats long after they were in full production. The last Scion Senior to be delivered was G-AETH; this aircraft was bought by the Air Ministry for experimental work in flying boat hull design. Assigned the military serial L9786, the aircraft had a half-scale Sunderland hull fitted directly under its fuselage and underwing floats. In this form, L9786 first flew with John Parker at the controls on 18 October 1939. The information gained from this trial led to the important Sunderland hull design change, which was adopted for the later Sunderland Mk III onwards, not to mention other data that was gathered to improve general performance.

Powered by four 950hp Bristol Pegasus X engines, K4774 was launched from Short Brothers' No. 3 Shop at Rochester on 14 October 1937. Over the next 48 hours, the aircraft completed its taxiing trials without difficulty and, on 16 October, with John Parker as pilot and his deputy Harold Piper (who became Short Brothers' chief test pilot on Parker's retirement in August 1945), K4774 made its first short flight. The aircraft needed little adjustment to continue flight trials but was instead returned to No. 3 Shop to have its wings swept back and a set of 1,010hp Pegasus XXII engines fitted. K4774 was back in the air on 7 March 1938 and was handed over to the MAEE one month later for service trials.

The two orders that Short Brothers received for the S.23 and S.25 – the former, for Imperial Airways – took priority, which was why the first S.23, *Canopus*, made its first flight 15 months before the Sunderland. Regardless, the first production batch of 11 Sunderland Mk Is (L2158 to L2168) under contract No. 533317/36 were already under construction, and the first production aircraft, L2158, was in the air on 21 April 1938. The last of this initial batch, L2168, was flown on 10 August 1938.

The Sunderland Mk I was marginally smaller than the S.23 Empire Boat. The wingspan was a foot shorter and the fuselage was almost three feet shorter, but the Sunderland's greater weight, increased power and better performance figures were superior to its civilian counterpart.

The impression that the Sunderland gave its first crews stayed with them for the rest of their careers, especially those who had experienced the cramped, cold and exposed days of the earlier biplane flying boats. One RAF pilot likened the Sunderland's cavernous interior to entering a cathedral; the cabin cockpit was 'sheer luxury' compared to the open cockpit flying boats, where one was exposed to the elements. Piloting this aircraft was like being on the bridge of a large ship, and equal comfort was afforded to the navigator, flight engineer and wireless operator. The rest bunks, a fully fitted kitchen and even a dining room were unheard of, and many thought of the Sunderland as a 'floating hotel'.

Full credit should go to the Short Brothers' designers, who had created an outstanding aircraft with emphasis on the crew being self-sufficient, especially when carrying out long-range flights. It was this foresight in particular that would prove invaluable for crews operating across the world.

The prototype S.25 Sunderland, K4774, on the slipway outside Short Brothers' No. 3 Shop at Rochester prior to the aircraft's taxiing trials in October 1937. (Via Martyn Chorlton)

K4774 emerging from No. 3 Shop following wing modification and uprated engines being fitted on 2 March 1938. Note in the background at least two Sunderland Mk Is already in an advanced state of production. (*Aeroplane*)

The Sunderland prototype at the Marine Aircraft Experimental Establishment (MAEE), Felixstowe, during its first Air Ministry trials in August 1938. (Via Martyn Chorlton)

Left: Short Scion Senior L9786 is launching at Rochester in November 1939, fitted with a half-scale Sunderland hull under the fuselage and similarly scaled-down sponsons under each wing. (Via Martyn Chorlton)

Below: Saro A.33 K4773 was the only other competitor in Specification R.2/33, which was comfortably won by the Sunderland following the demise of the A.33 in October 1938. (Via Martyn Chorlton)

The Short Sunderland Mk I

K4774 on 'the step' on the River Medway in 1938. (*Aeroplane*)

'The Bridge' of a Short Sunderland Mk I during early 1939. Note the gentle reminders 'Are All Hatches Closed?' and 'Flaps Must Not Be More Than (1/3) Out When Taking Off.' (*Aeroplane*)

DEBUNKING THE FLYING PORCUPINE MYTH

From the earliest days of service, the Sunderland was regarded as a heavily armed aircraft by the British and Empire press, even to the extent of using terms like 'Flying Fortress'. This was mainly due to the four belt-fed Browning .303 in guns in the tail turret. It is often overlooked that the three other guns were pan-fed .303 Vickers K guns, with a far lower rate of fire and small ammunition supply. It is unlikely that the Luftwaffe was impressed by this armament, having larger calibre, longer range and more powerful cannon in its machines.

The initial inadequate armament was boosted throughout the war with the addition of the mid upper turret and guns below the wings in the galley hatches. By the summer of 1943, the Sunderlands of Coastal Command faced the threat of long-range German fighters with a success rate that has become legendary. The Ju 88s of V/KG-40 patrolled in packs but, on more than one occasion, a lone Sunderland was able to fight off the assault and return to base. Perhaps the most frequently quoted battle is that of Flt Lt Colin Walker and crew of 461 Squadron flying EJ134 on 2 June 1943. As their patrol ended, eight Ju 88s were spotted and, in the ensuing 45-minute battle, they claimed three fighters shot down and several others damaged, although Luftwaffe records do not show a loss that day. One gunner on the Sunderland was mortally wounded and the aircraft so badly damaged it was beached at Praa Sands in Cornwall.

This is commonly cited as evidence for the Germans having nicknamed the Sunderland 'Fliegende Stachelswein' – the 'Flying Porcupine'. But how likely is it that the Germans gave the enemy such a name? And how likely is it that a German nickname would become well known in the UK?

Actually, the 1942 propaganda booklet *Coastal Command* describes the Sunderland as having 'a very wide range and an armament formidable enough for it to have been nicknamed "flying porcupine" by the Germans.' An earlier 1940 Christmas Quiz in *The Times* asked: 'What British aeroplane do the Germans call "Fliegende Stachelswein"?' Clearly, they expected their readers

The original 'Flying Porcupine'. 204 Squadron N9046, seen taking off in a shower of spray, was the aircraft flown by Flt Lt Phillips when it was involved in a battle with six Ju 88s over Norway, claiming one shot down. (Via Allan King and James Kightly)

would know the phrase. But just what incident was the question referring to? A clue lies even further back in an article on 11 September 1940 in *The Times* entitled 'A year's work of the RAF Coastal Command,' which stated: 'The Germans have a wholesome respect for them, and it is a pilot of more than average courage who would dare to tackle one unaided. With their guns sticking out at all angles, they seem to be able to fire in any direction. Because of their bristling armament, the Germans call them Fliegende Stachelswein.'

There were at least three incidents that the public would have known about in 1940 that proved the Sunderland's reputation for defence: two occurred during the Norwegian campaign, although perhaps the most dramatic was over the Mediterranean when Italian fighters attacked an aircraft with the war correspondent Alexander Clifford on board. Sunderland L5804 encountered three Macchi MC.200s on 28 July, claiming one shot down in a long battle described in some detail in Clifford's write-up for several newspapers.

Equally dramatic was an encounter on 3 April in Sunderland N9046, piloted by Flt Lt Frank Phillips. The Sunderland was on patrol off the Norwegian coast when it had a skirmish with two Ju 88s before running into six more. The official Air Ministry announcement stated: 'While engaged in patrol duties over the North Sea yesterday (Weds) afternoon, a flying boat of Coastal Command, RAF, encountered six enemy aircraft of the Junkers type. One of the latter was shot down and seen to fall into the sea. The remaining Junkers broke off the engagement and our aircraft resumed patrol.'

The stark statement hides the reality of the battle in which Cpl Lillie in the rear turret was cool enough to hold his fire until the Junkers was only 100 yards away. He watched his prey turn away sharply and spin into the sea. After the badly damaged Sunderland made it safely home, Flt Lt Phillips was awarded a DFC and Cpl Lillie the DFM.

It seems that N9046 was the original 'Flying Porcupine'. The incident was even used in adverts by Short Brothers soon after the attack.

Above left: The real German view of the Short Sunderland may be evident in this German published postcard from World War Two showing the flying boat as vulnerable to fighters. (Via Allan King and James Kightly)

Above right: The sting in the tail of the Sunderland was the FN.13 four-gun turret, which gave the Sunderland a reputation – in its home country, at least – as a well-defended aircraft. (Via Allan King and James Kightly)

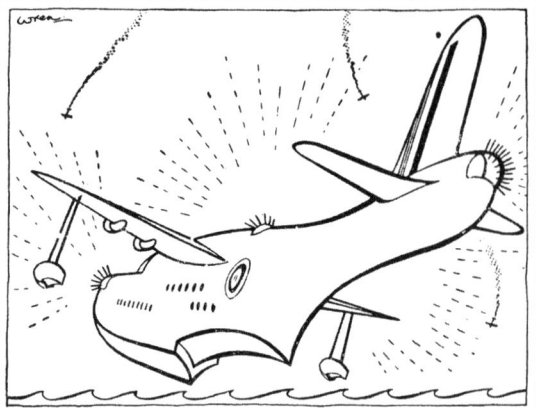

The 'Flying Porcupine' myth was popularly reinforced by cartoons such as Wrens, which appeared in *The Aeroplane* during World War Two. (*Aeroplane*)

Later that month, another Sunderland, N9025, fought off a Bf 110 over Molde Fjord. The 110 was later reported to have crashed as a result of the damage it received. But the Germans had their share of success against the Sunderlands over Norway, with L5799 lost on 7 April and L2167 lost on 9 April, both to a Bf 110.

Ironically, the British wartime public never got to see one reason the Germans might have regarded the Sunderland as a porcupine. For much of the war, Sunderlands operated with the dipole ASV radar aerials on the rear fuselage, making it look rather like a spiky hedgehog. But any images showing these aerials were censored in the British wartime press. Even today, these retouched photos are still often used and consequently continue to obscure the importance of radar in the U-boat battle. And there is no evidence that the aerials led German aircrew to call the Sunderlands 'Fliegende Stachelschwein'.

In 1940, the British needed to be able to celebrate how good their aircraft were – even if only when fighting off attackers. So, it seems someone just invented the name.

The impressive sight of an almost-complete Sunderland fuselage, leaving one of the jigs at the Short & Harland factory, on Queen's Island in Belfast. (Via Mike Hooks)

Chapter 2

The Sunderland Flying Boats of the Royal Air Force

From Aeronautical Engineering, *The Aeroplane*, 25 January 1939.

Flying boats intended for service with the Royal Air Force overseas, unlike aeroplanes produced for other military purposes, have to be designed as self-contained units able to operate far from their bases for long periods. The Royal Air Force have long been working to this end.

Technical difficulties were overcome comparatively early on. Range, for instance, is obviously a primary requirement. This was not difficult to get as extra fuel tanks could always be attached to the top of the hull or slung beneath the wings. The effect of this extra load, or 'overload' on the take-off was not really important as there is generally plenty of room for that purpose at sea.

Adequate seaworthiness has always been a feature of British-built flying boats. In fact, some people have argued that too much attention has been paid to this aspect at the expense of flying performance.

On the other hand, that general concession to hydrodynamic cleanliness, the use of wing-tip floats to provide lateral stability on the water instead of using sea-wings, or lateral sponsons on the side of the hull, probably has had the effect of making our boats vulnerable if put down on the water with drift in rough seas. However that may be, the present tendency is to retain the wing-tip float though efforts are being made to retract it into the wing or motor-nacelle.

Another snag of the pendant wing-float, though not so generally appreciated, is its effect on the stresses in the wing.

In this connection one has to consider the effect of a wing-tip float, probably 15ft. long and weighing 150lb. hung on struts some 10ft. below the wing.

The time is not yet but will undoubtedly come when the hulls of flying boats will be built of stainless steel. It will come, in fact, so soon as the plating can be used in gauges or thicknesses of such a size that local stiffening, such as by corrugation, will no longer be needed.

Problems of engine maintenance have been solved by making the flying boats carry the necessary cranes to lift the aero-motors in and out of their mountings and by the provision of suitable built-in working platforms.

The remaining difficulty has been the provision of adequate living quarters for the crew. Wonders have been done in providing accommodation in militant flying boats and as these got bigger so the quarters got better. Naturally, for service in the tropics the crew need all the space that can be given them, because a metal flying boat lying at anchor in tropic sun can become a pretty efficient sort of oven.

Consequently, with all these points in mind, we recently accepted with enthusiasm a chance to inspect one of the Sunderland flying boats of which a large number have been supplied to the R.A.F. who are flying them in service at home and in the Far East. A further series is now being built.

The Sunderland is, so far as we know, the largest flying boat in service with any Air Force in the World today. It is an all-metal boat seaplane with a cantilever monoplane wing and is driven by four Bristol Pegasus XXII air-cooled radials which provide a total of 4,040h.p. for take-off and a maximum power for level flight of 3,360h.p. at 6,250ft. The boat is normally loaded to 45,000lb. which on a wing area of just under 1,500sq. ft. works out at a wing loading of 30 lb. per sq. ft.

One might imagine that at such a high wing-loading the boat would be difficult to handle. Actually, in service, the boat behaves so well that the Royal Air Force habitually fly it at 50,000lb., which is quite a reasonable weight, in fact it comes out at something like 22 tons. The wing loading is then nearly 34lb. per sq. ft.

In spite of this the boat is being handled without difficulty by quite young and comparatively inexperienced pilots. In fairness to these officers we should explain that we are not suggesting that they are lacking in experience in relation to their seniority, merely that only a few years ago we should have thought that a boat of such enormous size could only be flown by pilots of many thousand hours' experience of that type of craft.

Mr. J. Lankester Parker, whose experience of testing large flying boats must be unequalled in England and probably in the World, told me something, while I was down looking over the Sunderland, which backs up this feature of easy handling in an interesting way. Recently, he had been discussing with other pilots the take-off of large landplanes.

The longest runway at Rochester aerodrome gives a run of 800 yards. There was some debate about whether it was enough. During the discussion Mr. Parker bethought himself of the 22-ton Sunderlands which he takes off and puts down on the Medway above Rochester Bridge without trouble. So he laid a ruler on the large-scale map of the river which hangs in his office. He then discovered that he has been taking off and putting down large flying boats, for all these years, the Sunderland included, from a piece of water whereon in no usable direction does the run exceed 800 yards.

This, as the stockbrokers say, is a bull point for a favourite argument of ours. In spite of their high wing-loading, the Sunderlands all have the Gouge dragless flap. This is an ingenious retractable portion of the underside trailing edge of the wing which can be slid backwards and downwards when taking off and alighting. The effect is not only to increase the Maximum Lift Coefficient (CL) of the wing, but also to increase its area without a very large increase of drag. Consequently, the alighting speed is very much less than one would expect from the wing loading.

In general form the Sunderland is a military version of the Empire flying boat but curiously enough in spite of its greater depth through the fuselage and greater weight, the Sunderland is just over a foot shorter in the span and 3ft. shorter over all.

The first thing that strikes a visitor on board is the general air of spaciousness. The door in the port side opens into a metal-floored compartment in which the most conspicuous object is the solid-seeming windlass to deal with the anchor chain or mooring gear.

In the extreme nose is a power-driven twin-gun turret. This can be slid backwards into the hull to provide an open cockpit for the handling of marine gear during the mooring operations. The sliding back of the turret also allows the erection of a mooring bollard on an extremely stout post. In the air this post is taken down and stowed inside the hull. Also when this is out of the way and the turret pushed forward into firing position, the nose portion of the hull can be opened up to provide a position for the bomb aimer.

Turning round to go aft one is faced by a flight of steps which lead up to what one might call the flight bridge, or pilots' compartment. Here are two seats side-by-side and in front of them are the normal stick-and-wheel controls and on the floor beyond them the adjustable rudder-bars. Between the seats and in front of the instrument board is the pulpit or battery of throttles and mixture controls. The Exactor hydraulic system of transmission is used for these.

The view from up here is very good and is improved by the fact that all the windows are flat. And, by making the flat surfaces into comparatively small panels, quite a good streamline shape has been obtained. In one window in front of each pilot is a circular cutting device so that he can make himself an exit in emergency.

Behind the pilots and a large hanging curtain is the space provided for the navigator and radio-operator. There is a large chart table on the starboard side and an armchair which slides out of the way beneath it. On the port side is the radio-operator's desk. Our eye was caught here by a looking glass placed so that the operator can watch the meters on the bulkhead behind him.

On the starboard side behind the navigator's table is the flight engineer's compartment. Here between the centre-section spars are all the various cocks and gauges for the control of the fuel supply. There is also a ladder from this compartment to the galley beneath.

The chain hoist for the removal or replacement of the motors is neatly stowed away here. The engineer also has the responsibility of looking after the steam-boiler heated by the exhaust which warms the incoming fresh air.

The fuel is normally carried outside the hull in the wings between the spars. There are three drum-shaped tanks each side of the hull. In an emergency, 52 per cent of the fuel can be jettisoned.

If we go forward again and down the stairs from the pilots' compartment we find that the lavatory is on the starboard side and that on the port is a passageway which leads to the wardroom. There is room in this passageway to hang coats, overalls, or oilskins. Two large suit cases are also stowed here. In the wardroom are two bunks and a table.

Immediately aft is the galley. As already mentioned there is a ladder from here to the flight engineer's compartment above. The galley is well provided with storage space, an ice chest for food, cooking equipment, a sink and draining board.

The galley is also used as a drogue operating station. The only means at present approved or provided for slowing down flying boats on the water is to heave overboard a drogue, a long canvas bucket without a bottom, on a length of rope. The drag of towing this through the water provides an effective brake. There are opening windows or ports in each side of the galley and a container below for the drogue and its rope so that all this gear can be handled conveniently.

Behind the galley are two compartments for the crew. Both have two bunks, one each side. In the first compartment the crew have to share the space with the main bomb load. a very ingenious system is provided to get the bombs out of here into the air but it cannot be described in detail. Provision is also made in the port side of the hull for the removal of two large panels so that a complete spare aero-motor can be taken on board.

There is a metal roof to the galley and on top of this are stored the smoke-floats. These make a heavy smoke when dropped on the water and so provide useful information about the direction and force of the wind. Access to the storage place of these floats is by manhole from the engineers' compartment or by catwalk from the midship gun positions.

Behind the second crew's compartment are the two platforms for the midship guns. The catwalk from these to the metal roof over the galley has previously been mentioned. Normally, the openings for the midship guns are closed by neatly fitting hatches, but these can be taken inside and the gun is erected on a pillar mounting. Some protection from the slipstream is provided by a cowling on the forward side.

A catwalk along the bottom of the hull leads one to the power-driven gun-turret in the tail. Sitting up here one was impressed by the attention given to details. Besides having his own man-sized electric

An early production Sunderland Mk I banks alongside the prototype K4774; photographed from the port bomb hatch. (Flight)

light, the gunner is kept warm or cool by an individual supply of fresh air (warm or cold), the amount of which he can regulate. On the way up one passes the hatch in the bottom of the hull which can be lifted to provide an opening for the camera.

Large numbers of these boats have been sent out to the East and so all the portholes or window-lights are provided with curtains. A system of cowls has also been worked out to improve the interior ventilation when afloat.

The second production Sunderland Mk I, L2159, which first flew on 4 May 1938. After brief spells with the MAEE and 209 Squadron, L2159 joined 230 Squadron. While the Sunderland was undergoing maintenance at the Flying Boat Servicing Unit (FBSU) at Greenock, the flying boat was destroyed in a Luftwaffe raid on 7 May 1941. (Via Martyn Chorlton)

The starboard Bristol Pegasus XXII 1,050hp engines, driving de Havilland (Hamilton) three-bladed two-pitch propellers, tick over while taxiing at Felixstowe in early 1938. (*Aeroplane*)

The 'bridge' of an early production Sunderland. The cockpit of the Sunderland evolved with the aircraft, which by the time the later Mk Vs had arrived in the 1950s, were barely recognisable compared to their 1930s' counterparts. (Via Martyn Chorlton)

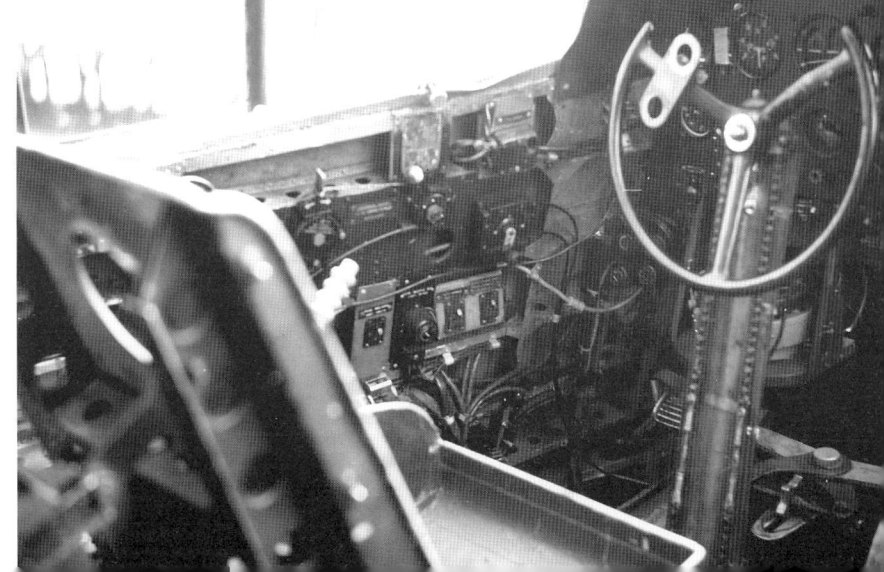

The pilot's position in an early Sunderland Mk I, still in need of some refinement. (Via Martyn Chorlton)

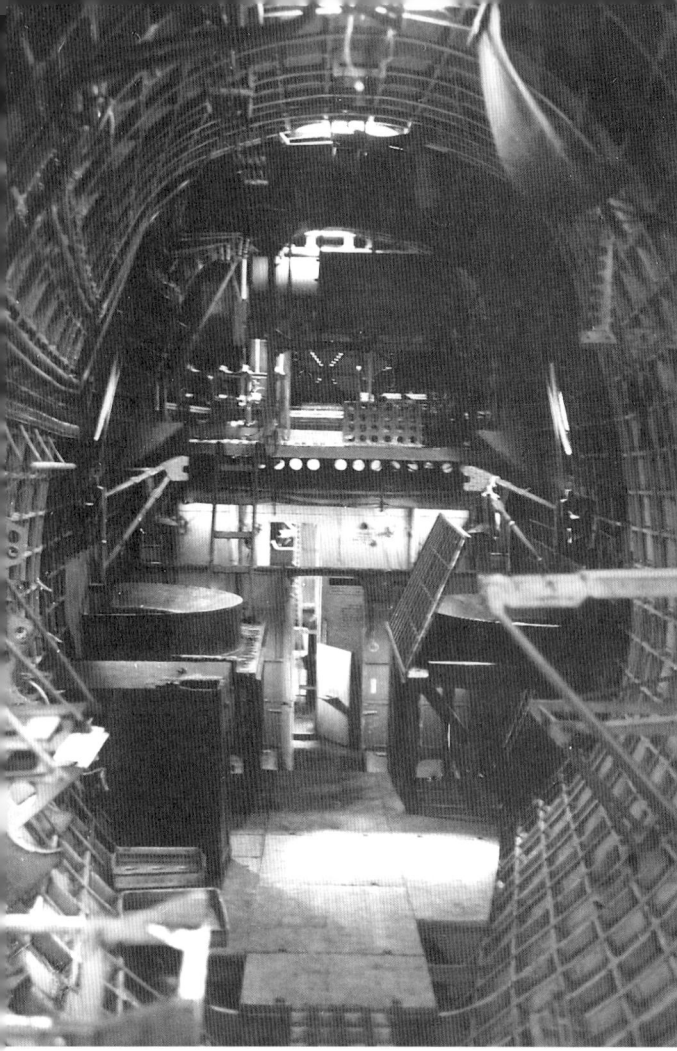

Left: The cavernous 'cathedral-like' interior of the Sunderland looking forward from the rear fuselage. The galley and 'dining room' is down below rising to the first floor, where flares and smoke floats were stored. (Via Martyn Chorlton)

Below: Sunderland Mk I L5799 of 210 Squadron is drawing a crowd at Pembroke Dock for the Empire Air Day in May 1939. The flying boat was shot down during a running dogfight with an He 111 off Bergen on 8 April 1940, killing all nine crew on board. (Via Martyn Chorlton)

Aerodynamics

Aerodynamically, the layout of the Sunderland differs but little from that of the Empire Boat. The form of the hull has been modified to meet military requirements. The installation, for instance of a gun-turret in the extreme stern, has modified the shape of the hull around the tailplane and fin. There is also some departure from the rectangular cross-section of the Empire Boat.

The most interesting feature of the Sunderland is the novel form of the bottom of the hull. As Mr. H. M. Gamer disclosed in his lecture at the conference of the Lilienthal-Gesellschaft last October, a great deal of drag is caused by the steps which are necessary on the bottom of the hull to provide a good take-off. He then indicated that there was a very good chance of fairing the main step in, or at any rate of making the discontinuity on the bottom of a hull of such form as to reduce the air drag very considerably.

This has not been done on the Sunderland. The main step is of V shape in plan with the apex of the V pointing aft. This is probably to improve stability and prevent porpoising. Instead of ending in a second or rear step the planing bottom terminates in a vertical knife-edge which sweeps up into the rounded portion of the hull which extends out to the tail.

Thought of in terms of big flying boats and the usual British arrangement of two steps the arrangement certainly seems novel. But when one recalls the shape of the earlier American flying boats, particularly the NC flying boats which made the first crossing of the Atlantic, one can see that this single main step and vertical stern is a logical development of the earlier practice. Practically all seaplane floats have single main steps and a vee-shaped planing bottom which ends in a stern-post.

The idea seems to work well in practice. And in fact, the Sunderland is faster than the Empire flying boat. Anybody who is interested in this particular subject would do well to look up our report of Mr. Garner's lecture in *The Aeroplane* of 16 November 1938, and to study the pictures.

Excellent view of the stepped hull of a Sunderland flying boat, which in this case belongs to 10 Squadron RAAF. (Via Martyn Chorlton)

K4774 spent most of its flying career with the MAEE at Felixstowe, before it was damaged in an accident on 13 February 1942. It was not struck off charge (SOC) until 21 June 1947. (Via Martyn Chorlton)

The Structure

Generally speaking, the structure of the Sunderland is that of the Empire Boat. The skin plating of the wings and hull is all assembled with 'joggled' joints and countersunk riveting to make the skin as smooth as possible.

The hull and wings are plated with Alclad Na 24 ST or, in the later types, with Alclad Na 23 ST. Much Hiduminium RR 56 is used in the structure of the hull and wings.

The wing is built around a main box-spar. This consists or two girder members joined with sturdy transverse members and the whole cross-braced in the transverse plane with steel tie-rods.

The girder members themselves have flanges of extruded light alloy which are machined to the proper taper and form on a specially constructed milling machine. The webs of these girders are made of diagonal struts built up of extruded tubes and extruded sections ingeniously designed so that only a simple machining operation is needed to make suitable connecting pieces.

To ensure interchange-ability the wings are assembled to a master centre-section. Because of the large amount of light steel girder work in this jig it is known in the works as the 'Westminster' jig.

The main trusses or girder members of the centre-section are also built to a master jig and are then sent back to the Frame Shop for incorporation in the main spar-frames. By virtue of this arrangement rigid control is ensured and as a result in spite of the enormous size of the wings they can be assembled to the boat with the minimum of trouble.

The metal-plated gouge flaps which fit so snugly beneath the trailing edge of the wing are driven electrically. A Rotax high-speed motor drives a series of screw-jacks through shafting.

The flaps are carried by a series of rollers on arms that project from the wing into the flap. These rollers run in curved channels built into the flaps. The grooves in which the rollers run have to be machined with great accuracy, as any 'flats' on the surface would cause them to jam. These curved channels are milled out of a solid bar, after this has been bent to shape.

As with the Empire Boats, the hulls are built in a gantry, the right way up and plated in position, much as a ship is built, but whereas work on most ships begins with the laying of the keel from which the frames or ribs are built up, in the building of the Sunderland and the Empire Boats the frames are built first in horizontal jigs. These jigs are of very simple form and really consist of large tables on which the 'lines' have been laid out. When the frames are complete they are lifted out and put in a

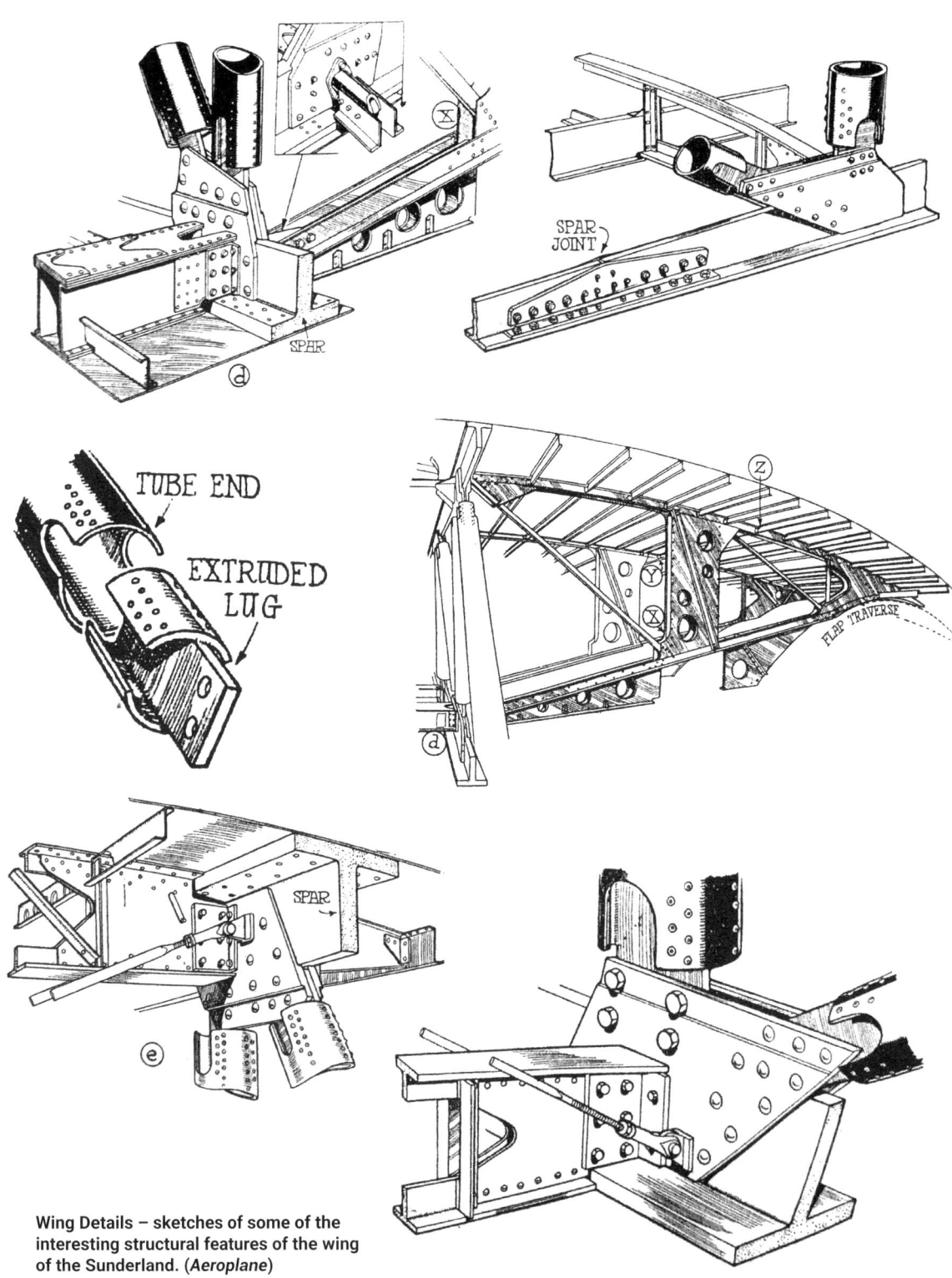

Wing Details – sketches of some of the interesting structural features of the wing of the Sunderland. (*Aeroplane*)

gantry. A keel and keelsons are then built in and the Z-shaped stringers, to which the plating is riveted, are put in place.

The motor-nacelles are of straightforward shell construction, built around circular frames. The mounting ring of the Bristol Pegasus is bolted directly to the stiff circular channel of light alloy which forms the nose of the nacelle. To add the necessary stiffness, strong radial ribs are built into the nose the nacelle.

The fuel tanks are of the same successful design used in the Empire Boat. The simple design of drum used, in which the flat top and bottom discs are tied together by steel tie-rods, results in an extraordinarily low weight per gallon of capacity. In the Empire Boats we believe that this figure worked out at about 3lb per gallon.

The fuel tanks are carried in the motor-nacelles, but the oil coolers are in the leading edges of the wing, where by a suitable arrangement of inlet and outlet slots, a steady stream of cooling air is available at low cost in drag.

An interesting feature of the motor installation is the auxiliary power unit driven by a small petrol motor which is mounted in the leading edge of the starboard wing. This provides the power necessary for refuelling, pumping out the bilges or charging the batteries.

The wing-tip floats are built of light alloy in the usual way, with keelsons and transverse frames and a skin of light alloy sheet. Each watertight compartment is provided with means for pumping out the bilge water.

The cantilever tail unit is built like that of the Empire Boat.

The third production Mk I, L2160, first flew on 18 May 1938 and within five days was on strength with 209 Squadron. The aircraft remained with the squadron for a few weeks before being passed to 230 Squadron and christened *Selangor*. Service with 228 Squadron and 4 Operational Training Unit (OTU) followed before the flying boat became airframe number 3372M in 1942. (*Aeroplane*)

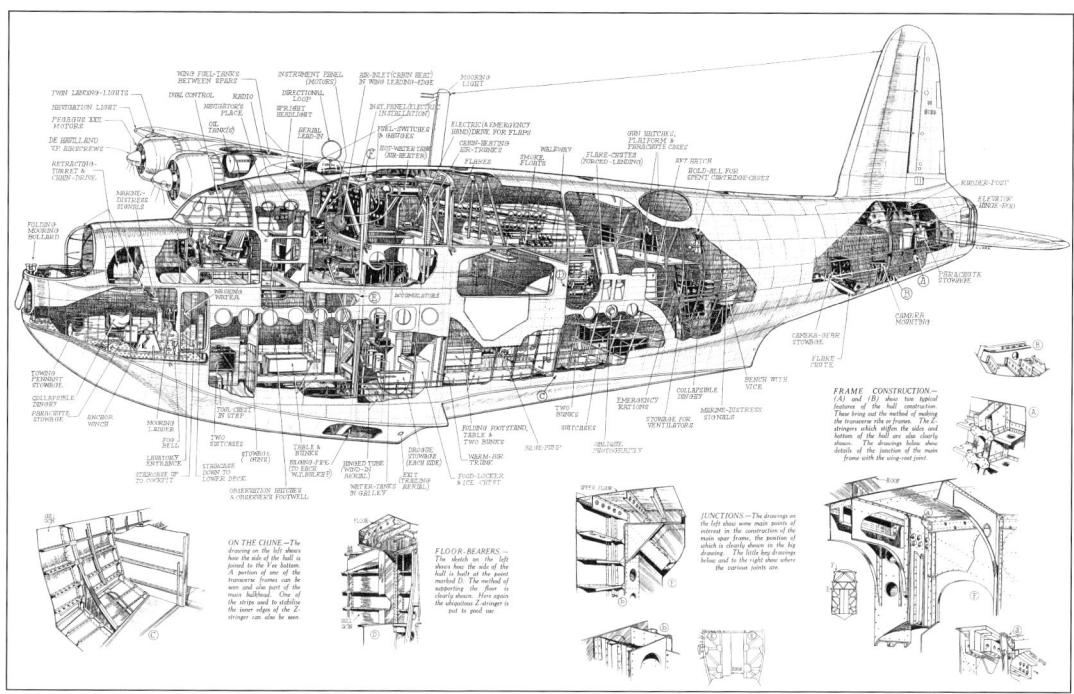

The RAF Sunderland I Flying Boat (four 1,010hp British Pegasus XXII motors).

SPECIFICATIONS
(Sunderland Mk I as known in 1939)

Weights – Empty, 28,290lb; Crew, 1,400lb; Fuel, 11,400lb; Oil, 830lb; Disposable, 16,410lb; Loaded, 45,700lb; Maximum Overload, 49, 870lb; Wing Loading, 30lb per sq ft; Power Loading, 11.5lb per hp; Span Loading, 3 to 6lb per sq ft.

Performance – (At 45,700lb) – Maximum Speed, 210mph at 6,250ft; Cruising Speed on 65% power, 178mph at 5,750ft; Stalling Speed at sea-level, 80mph; Take-off, 23 seconds with 10mph wind; Normal Range, 1,670 sea-miles; Maximum Range, 2,500 sea-miles; Initial Rate of Climb, 1,200ft per minute; Service Ceiling, 20,500ft.

Chapter 3

Mass Producing the Sunderland

The Factories

Rochester – Building military flying boats in peacetime was a leisurely activity compared to supplying the vibrant Imperial Airways with Empire Boats. Therefore, when orders came in from both the military (for the Sunderland) and for more civilian C-Class Empire Boats, the latter took priority in 1937. However, this did not mean that Short Brothers would not display any foresight with regard to the Sunderland and, before the prototype was in the air, the first production batch of 11 Mk Is (L2158 to L2168) was already well under way.

Before 1938 was over, another ten Mk Is (L5798 to L5807) had been delivered and, by now, all eyes had turned towards Europe, as another world war beckoned. Further military orders were now overtaking the civilian ones as the RAF tried to achieve the 'expansion period' figures placed upon it. At the outbreak of World War Two, the contracts Short Brothers accepted were doubling in size and would continue to grow until they peaked in early 1943, when an order for 75 Mk IIIs was received. By this time, Short Brothers (Rochester & Bedford) Ltd had been taken over by the government, coming under the control of the Ministry of Aircraft Production in March 1943. The surviving brother, Oswald, had resigned from the chairmanship in January but would remain as life president until his death in December 1969.

Including the Sunderland prototype, 331 were built at Rochester, made up of 74 Mk Is, 23 Mk IIs, 186 Mk IIIs and 47 Mk Vs. The last batch of 28 Mk Vs was delivered to the RAF in June 1946, leaving the Rochester plant to continue with conversion work to civilian configurations, the vast majority of them destined for BOAC.

By 1947, the Harland & Wolff shares within Short & Harland Ltd in Belfast were purchased by the government and, from November of that year, the company as a whole became known as Short Brothers & Harland Ltd. Rochester then fell into decline as work was systematically transferred across the water to Belfast. By 1948, this once vibrant and crucially important centre for aircraft production was closed down.

Belfast – The relatively new arm of Short Brothers was formed in June 1936 under the joint control of Short Brothers (Rochester & Bedford) Ltd and Harland & Wolff Ltd. A new factory was built on land at Queen's Island, Belfast, for Short & Harland Ltd, with landplane production operating from Sydenham Airport and flying boats using Belfast Lough and later Musgrave Channel.

The main production during World War Two was the Short Stirling but 133 Sunderlands were also built in Belfast: 15 were Mk IIs, 71 Mk IIIs and 47 Mk Vs, the last of which, SZ599, was flown off the Lough on 14 June 1946. Short & Harland Ltd also gained work converting five Sunderlands to civilian configuration for Argentina and Paraguay. Twenty-six Sandringham conversions followed, including three Sandringham 2s, two Sandringham 3s, four Sandringham 4s, nine Sandringham 5s, five Sandringham 6s and three Sandringham 7s.

The factory is the only plant that produced the Sunderland to survive today, and it is now under the control of Bombardier.

Dumbarton – Formed as a joint venture with William Denny & Bros Ltd, Blackburn Aircraft Ltd established new factories at Castle Road and Barge Park, Dumbarton in October 1936. This busy plant was responsible for building the Shark, Botha and B-20 experimental flying boat before accepting a contract to build the first of 250 Short Sunderlands.

There were 15 Mk Is, five Mk IIs, 170 Mk IIIs and 60 Mk Vs built at Dumbarton. The first to leave the plant was the Mk II prototype, T9083, which was flown from the River Leven, next to the factory that flows into the River Clyde. All other aircraft were towed five miles downriver to Rhu/Helensburgh, the home of the MAEE throughout World War Two. The last Sunderland to leave Dumbarton was Mk V VB889, which was completed on 25 October 1945 and flew out to Wig Bay on 8 November 1945.

The Dumbarton factory continued to build aircraft components into the 1950s but, in August 1960, Blackburn (Dumbarton) Ltd was closed.

Windermere – The site of Short Brothers' repair and manufacturing factory was at Calgarth Park, one mile northwest of Windermere on the edge of White Cross Bay and was open by September 1942. Construction of the factory on 28 acres of wood and farmland was swift. The main hangar had the distinction of being the biggest unsupported span in the country and was capable of housing nine Sunderlands. Along the main road to Troutbeck Bridge, a prefabricated village was also constructed. The village contained 243 bungalows, plus several hostels, to accommodate the influx of skilled workers who were transferred from all over the country. The plant, which would eventually employ nearly 2,000 workers, included many local people trained by Short.

In total, 35 (DP176 to DP200 and EJ149 to EJ158) Sunderlands, all Mk IIIs, were built under two contracts, with the last aircraft being delivered by July 1944. Repair work continued into 1945, but, post-war, the factory saw a rapid decline and it was completely abandoned by the early 1950s.

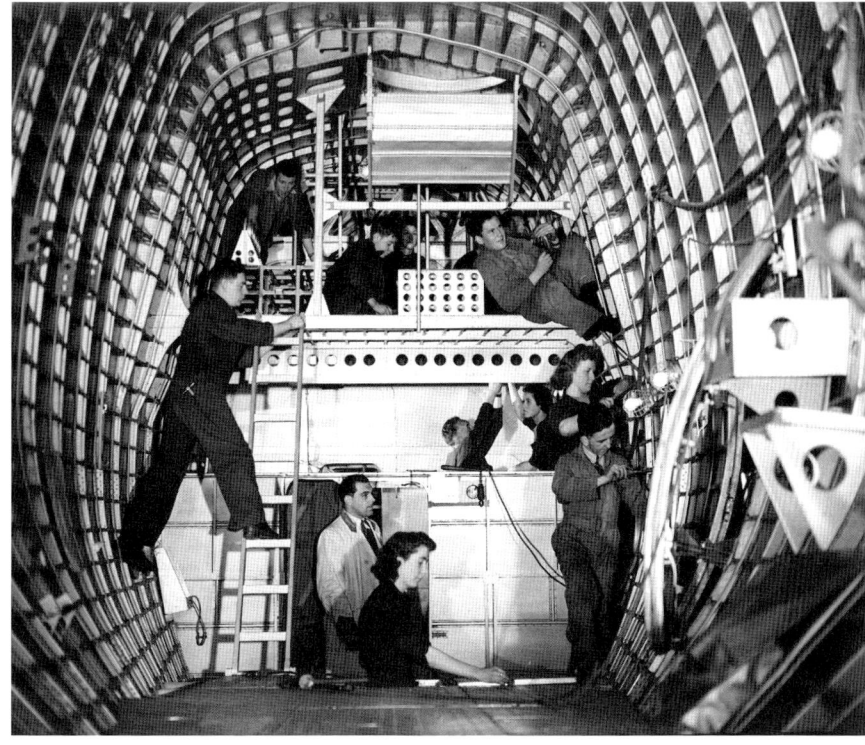

An excellent 'stage-managed' photograph of workers at Short Brothers' Rochester factory, working on a Sunderland Mk III. The ratio of women to men would steadily rise as the war progressed. (Via Allan King)

A Short Sunderland hull in a jig during assembly at Rochester in April 1938. The steel girder jigs formed accurate positions for the keel, top board and the rear frame with scaffolding mounted clear of the aircraft. (Via Allan King)

An early Sunderland nearing completion in No. 3 Shop at Rochester. The beaching trolley has been fitted, the wing supports removed and the tail will shortly be lowered. Note the rather rudimentary arrangement with a ladder to gain access to the wings and hull. (Via Allan King)

A vast one-piece Sunderland Mk II fuselage after being lifted from a jig at Belfast. (Via Allan King)

Sunderland assembly stages in the main hangar at the Windermere Works during early 1943. At the front right, the aircraft is almost complete, while on the one behind it, the wings have only just been fitted to the aircraft and props are still in place. The Sunderland at the front left is between these two stages. (Peter Greetham)

MUSGRAVE CHANNEL (BELFAST HARBOUR), BELFAST CITY

Located 500m west of Belfast City Airport, flying boats made use of the extensive Musgrave Channel with Belfast Harbour from 1928 to 1949. Civilian aircraft used it prior to and post-World War Two, with the RAF and quite possibly occasional US Navy machines using it during wartime. The landing area is described as being in a north-south direction and was over 4,500ft in length.

At least five Sunderland Mk Vs are dwarfed by the massive Harland & Wolff cranes whilst moored in Musgrave Channel in 1945. (*Aeroplane*)

The Production

Short Sunderland prototype delivered to MAEE in April 1938 to Contract 351564/34: K4774.

11 Short Sunderland Mk Is delivered between April and August 1938 by Short, Rochester, to Contract No. 533317/36: L2158 to L2168.

Ten Short Sunderland Mk Is delivered between September and November 1938 by Short, Rochester, to Contract No. 533317/36: L5798 to L5807.

Three Short Sunderland Mk Is delivered in February 1939 by Short, Rochester, to Contract No. 774293/38: N6133, N6135 and N6138.

18 Short Sunderland Mk Is delivered between March and October 1939 by Short, Rochester, to Contract No. 774293/38: N9020 to N9030 and N9044 to N9050.

12 Short Sunderland Mk Is delivered between September 1939 and April 1940 by Short, Rochester, to Contract No. B985038/39: P9600 to P9606 and P9620 to P9624.

20 Short Sunderland Mk Is delivered between July 1940 and March 1941 by Short, Rochester, to Contract No. 18347/37: T9040 to T9050 and T9070 to T9078.

15 Short Sunderland Mk IIs delivered between November 1941 and July 1942 by Blackburn, Dumbarton, to Contract No. 37753/39: T9083 to T9090 and T9109 to T9115.

23 Short Sunderland Mk IIs delivered between May and December 1941 by Short, Rochester, to Contract No. B.18347/39: W3976 to W3998.

38 Short Sunderland Mk IIIs delivered between January and June 1942 by Short, Rochester, to Contract No. B.18347/39: W3999 to W4037.

Five Short Sunderland Mk IIs delivered between May and July 1942 by Blackburn Aircraft, Dumbarton, to Contract No. B.37753/39: W6000 to W6004.

29 Short Sunderland Mk IIIs delivered between August and November 1942 by Blackburn Aircraft, Dumbarton, to Contract No. B.37753/39: W6005 to W6033.

15 Short Sunderland Mk IIs delivered between January and December 1942 by Short Brothers & Harland, Belfast, to Contract No. B.76674/40: W6050 to W6064.

Ten Short Sunderland Mk IIIs delivered between January and April 1943 by Short Brothers & Harland, Belfast, to Contract No. B.76674/40: W6065 to W6068 and W6075 to W6080.

40 Short Sunderland Mk IIIs delivered between December 1942 and June 1943 by Blackburn Aircraft, Dumbarton, to Contract No. B37753/39: DD828 to DD867.

25 Short Sunderland Mk IIIs delivered between September 1942 and January 1944 by Short, Windermere, to Contract No. 234/SAS/40/C20B: DP176 to DP200.

25 Short Sunderland Mk IIIs delivered between June and October 1942 by Short, Rochester, to Contract No. B78939/40: DV956 to DV980.[1]

20 Short Sunderland Mk IIIs delivered between May and October 1943 by Short Brothers & Harland, Belfast, to Contract No. 76674/40: DV985 to DV994 and DW104 to DW113.

15 Short Sunderland Mk IIIs delivered between April and December 1942 by Short, Rochester, to Contract No. B78939/40: EJ131 to EJ145.

Ten Short Sunderland Mk IIIs delivered between February and July 1944 by Short, Windermere, to Contract No. 234/SAS/40C20B: EJ149 to EJ158.

Ten Short Sunderland Mk IIIs delivered between October 1943 and February 1944 by Short Brothers & Harland, Belfast, to Contract No. 76674/40: EJ163 to EJ172.

25 Short Sunderland Mk IIIs delivered between June and October 1943 by Blackburn Aircraft, Dumbarton, to Contract No. B37753/39: EK572 to EK596.

50 Short Sunderland Mk IIIs delivered between December 1942 and August 1943 by Short, Rochester, to Contract No. B78939/40: JM659 to JM689 and JM704 to JM722.

45 Short Sunderland Mk IIIs delivered between August 1943 and November 1944 by Short, Rochester, to Contract No. A/C 2538: (some converted to Mk V/GR.V) ML725 to ML744 and ML777 to ML801.

25 Short Sunderland Mk IIIs delivered between February 1944 and September 1944 by Short Brothers and Harland, Belfast, to Contract No. A/C 2227: (several converted to GR.5) ML807 to ML831.

50 Short Sunderland Mk IIIs delivered between October 1943 and May 1944 by Blackburn Aircraft, Dumbarton, to Contract No. A/C 2228/C20(B): (several converted to GR.5) ML835 to ML884.

Two Short Seaford Mk I prototypes built by Short in 1944: MZ269 and MZ271.

25 Short Sunderland Mk IIIs delivered between May and August 1944 by Blackburn Aircraft, Dumbarton, to Contract No. A/C 2228/C20(B): NJ170 to NJ194.

25 Short Sunderland Mk IIIs and Vs (from NJ259) delivered between September 1944 and June 1945 by Short Brothers & Harland, Belfast, to Contract No. A/C 2227: NJ253 to NJ277.

30 Short Sunderland Mk Vs delivered between November 1944 and June 1945 by Short, Rochester, to Contract No. A/C 2226: PP103 to PP132.

Ten Short Sunderland Mk IIIs delivered between August and October 1944 by Blackburn Aircraft, Dumbarton, to Contract No. A/C 2228/C20(B): PP135 to PP144.

---

1   DV959 built as SD123 to Contract No. 78939/40 and DV960 built as SD124 to Contract No. 78939/40.

Sunderland Mk III ML866 in the foreground of the main assembly shed at Short Brothers in Belfast. ML866 was actually built by Blackburn Aircraft at Dumbarton, so it is most likely that the aircraft was here to be modified to Mk V standard. (Via Allan King)

20 Short Sunderland Mk Vs delivered between October 1944 and February 1945 by Blackburn Aircraft, Dumbarton, to Contract No. A/C 2228/C20(B): PP145 to PP164.

Ten Short Sunderland Mk Vs delivered between June and November 1945 by Short, Rochester, to Contract No. A/C 2226: RN264 to RN273.

30 Short Sunderland Mk Vs delivered between February and October 1945 by Blackburn, Dumbarton, to Contract No. A/C2228/C20(B): RN277 to RN306.

28 (from an original order of 40 aircraft) Short Sunderland Mk Vs delivered by Short Brothers and Harland, Belfast between June 1945 and June 1946, to Contract No. 4067: SZ559 to SZ584, SZ598 and SZ599 (SZ600 to SZ611 cancelled).

One Short Sunderland Mk V delivered in December 1945, to Contract No. A/C 2226: TX293.

Ten Short Sunderland GR.5s delivered between August and November 1945 by Blackburn, Dumbarton, to Contract No. A/C 2228/C20(B): VB880 to VB889

Cancelled Contracted Batches

AX936 to AX950 (15); AX973 to AX997 (25); NE836 to NE885 (50 Mk III); NN841 to NN990 (50 Mk IV); NP100 to NP149 (50 Mk IV); SZ600 and SZ611 (2); TK440 to TK468 (29 Mk IV); TK482 to TK512 (31 Mk IV); TW774 to TW803 (30); TX294 to TX296 (3). Total 285 Aircraft.

Marks Converted to Mk V Standard

DP191, DP195, DP198–DP200, DV976, EJ152, EJ153, EJ155, EJ167, EJ171, EJ172, EK579, EK592, JM667, JM681, JM714, JM715, JM717–JM720, ML739, ML741, ML745, ML747, ML757, ML761, ML763–ML765, ML768, ML772, ML778–ML781, ML783, ML784, ML807, ML809, ML812, ML814–ML821, ML824, ML826–ML828, ML838, ML840, ML866, ML872, ML873, ML875, ML877, ML878, ML881, ML882, NJ170-NJ172, NJ176, NJ177, NJ179, NJ180, NJ182, NJ187, NJ188-NJ194, NJ253–NJ255, NJ257, NJ258, PP137, PP143, PP144

Suppliers of Accessories

Accles and Pollock Ltd (stainless and mild steel tubes); Amal Ltd (pressure-reducing valves); Bakelite Ltd (Bakelite sheet); Birmingham Battery and Metal Co Ltd (copper tube); Bell's Asbestos and Eng Supplies Co Ltd (Asbestos goods); Birmabright Ltd (Birmabright tubes); James Bright and Co Ltd (Duralumin, bar, sheet and tubes, etc.); Bowden Engineers Ltd (Bowden clips); The Breeze Corp of Gt Britain Ltd (electrical fittings); Bristol Aeroplane Co Ltd (engines); The British Aluminium Co (aluminium sheets, tubes and ingots); British Celanese Ltd (Celastoid sheeting); British Insulated Cables Ltd (electric cables); British Thomson-Houston Ltd (electrical equipment); Brown Bros Ltd (AGS parts); Bruntons (Musselburgh) Ltd (streamline wires and tie rods); Callender's Cable and Construction Co (electric cables); L. Cameron and Son (Camloy sheet); The Cork Mfg Co (Langite sheets and cork floats); Cornercroft Ltd (pressings); Dashwood Engineering Ltd (machined parts, bolts, etc); De Bergue Patents Ltd (patent rivets); The Dunlop Rubber Co Ltd (tyres and wheels); Ellison Insulations Ltd (Tufnol bars and tubes); Exactor Control Co Ltd (throttle controls); Firth-Vickers Stainless Steels Ltd (stainless steel bars); Flexo Plywood Industries Ltd (aircraft plywood); Gallay Ltd (heaters); J. J. Habershon and Sons (stainless steel and carbon steel sheets and strips); High Duty Alloys Ltd (aluminium alloy sheets, etc.); The Hoffmann Manufacturing Co Ltd (ball and roller bearings); Wm. Jessop and Sons Ltd (stainless steel bars, forgings, sheets, etc); Lissen Ltd (machining special parts); Manganese Bronze and Brass Co Ltd (Oilite bushes); John Marston Ltd (oil-coolers); May and Baker Ltd (Rhodoid); M.R.C. Ltd (Teleflex controls); The Mollart Engineering Co Ltd (ball joints); Northern Aluminium Co Ltd (aluminium alloy sheets, bars, etc, and extrusions); S. E. Opperman Ltd (machining and assembly); Power Flexible Tubing Co Ltd (Avioflexus tubing); Renold and Coventry Chain Co Ltd (chain): Reynolds Tube Co Ltd (aluminium alloy sheets, tubes, bars, extrusions, etc); Robertson Coolers Ltd (oil-coolers); Rotax Ltd (electrical equipment); Rotherham and Sons Ltd (drain taps, etc); George Salter and Co Ltd (springs); Serck Radiators Ltd (radiator tubes); Superflexit Ltd (Superflexit tubes): Simmonds Aerocessories Ltd (Simmonds nuts): Skefko Ball Bearing Co Ltd (ball and roller bearings); Smiths Aircraft Instruments (instruments); Smith's Stamping Works Ltd (light alloy stampings); Sperry Gyroscope Co Ltd (shock absorbers and Sperry equipment); Spring Washers Ltd (spring washers); Sterling Metals Ltd (castings); J. Stone and Co Ltd (light alloy rivets and Elektron castings); Recalemit Ltd (greasers); Technical Rubber Co Ltd (petrol-resisting rubber); H. Terry and Co Ltd (Anglepoise lamps); Triplex Safety Glass Co Ltd (aero glass); Tuck and Co Ltd (packing rings); Vokes Ltd (oil cleaner); The Weston Electrical Instrument Co Ltd (pyrometers); Whitely Products Ltd (rubber chord); Wilkinson Rubber Linatex Ltd (Linatex rubber).

"THE SUNDERLAND"
ONE OF THE NEW FLYING BOATS DESIGNED AND BUILT FOR THE ROYAL AIR FORCE
BY
SHORT BROS. (ROCHESTER & BEDFORD) LTD. ROCHESTER

Above: The Detail Shop was the main work area at the Windermere Works and shows the essentially hand-built nature of the aircraft. In the foreground are wooden bucks for making engine nacelles. From the roof hangs a propaganda poster showing an RAF fighter swooping over a downed German aircraft. The poster reads 'The RAF are doing a fine job – this plant will help them finish it.' (Peter Greetham)

Below left: Sunderland maintenance line at Short Brothers & Harland's large hangar in Belfast. The aircraft on the right have all seen operational service and are either being serviced or upgraded to Mk Vs. (Via Allan King)

Below right: Sunderland Mk Is T9048 'N' of 228 Squadron (foreground) and L2160 'X' of 230 Squadron are moored in Messinia Bay, Kalamata, during the evacuation of RAF personnel from Greece. (Via *Aeroplane*)

Chapter 4

The Queen of the Air Rules the Waves!

Pre-war build-up

The very first Sunderland Mk I to enter RAF service was the second production aircraft, L2159. In the hands of Flt Lt W. A. Hughes and manned by a 210 Squadron crew, the flying boat left Pembroke Dock on 9 June 1938, bound for the Far East. The route taken was Gibraltar, Malta, Alexandria, Habbaniya, Bahrain, Karachi, Gwalior, Calcutta, Rangoon, Mergui, and finally arriving in Singapore on 22 June. It was here that L2159 was handed over to 230 Squadron to be joined by L2160 on 4 July, which took the same route and was flown by Sqn Ldr A. M. Watts-Read.

The remainder of the first production batch (L2161 to L2168) was delivered to 210 Squadron at Pembroke Dock between June and August 1938, as temporary replacements for the unit's Short Singapores. 230 Squadron continued to gain strength in the Far East while a second UK-based unit was being prepared. 202 Squadron was next in line, receiving N6135 and N9021 in April 1939, but this was to be short-lived as the aircraft were transferred to 228 Squadron instead. 202 Squadron would not become fully re-equipped with the Sunderland until December 1941. Once 228 Squadron had reached its full establishment of Sunderlands, the unit was posted to Alexandria in June 1939.

The fourth and final pre-war Sunderland unit was 204 Squadron, based at Mount Batten, which began replacing its Saro Londons during June and July 1939.

Sunderland Mk I L2163 of 210 Squadron keeps a close eye on Canadian Troop Convoy 6 (T.C.6) in 1941, bound for Greenock. (Via Martyn Chorlton)

L2161 *Negri Sembilan* at Nancowry, Nicobar Islands, Indian Ocean, on 12 January 1939. (Via Martyn Chorlton)

Let battle commence

When World War Two broke out in September 1939, the RAF had 40 Sunderlands on strength within its four squadrons, although two had already been written off in accidents.

The honour of flying the first Sunderland operation of World War Two fell to Flt Lt A. S. Ainslie in L2165 'B' of 210 Squadron. The sortie, on 3 September, was a convoy escort patrol covering shipping routes into Milford Haven. Awarded the DFC in February 1940, Ainslie was lost on operations on 29 June 1940. Flying Sunderland Mk I N9026, it is presumed that the flying boat was shot down off the south west coast of Ireland. South African-born Ainslie and eight of his crew are commemorated on the Runnymede Memorial.

A fifth Sunderland squadron was in the planning stages before the start of the war, but this was to serve with the Royal Australian Air Force (RAAF). 10 (General Reconnaissance) Squadron RAAF was formed at Point Cook, Victoria, on 1 July 1939, under the command of Sqn Ldr L. Lachal. The original plan was for the new squadron to operate from a brand-new flying boat station at Rathmines, New South Wales, equipped with the Sunderland. Seven pilots were sent to England to begin conversion training, initially on the Short Singapore at Calshot, before ferrying their brand new Sunderlands back to Australia. The handful of pilots were joined by a growing party and were later attached to 210 Squadron for familiarisation training. By September, 10 Squadron received its first Sunderlands with plans in motion to ferry the first three back to Australia in October. However, on 8 October, Sqn Ldr Lachal received orders that 10 Squadron RAAF was to remain in the UK for active service and, on 10 October, the unit flew its first operational flight in N9049.

On 3 January 1940, 10 Squadron came under the control of 15 Group, Coastal Command, flying its first official 'war' operation on 6 February, which was the first all-Australian-crewed aircraft operation of World War Two. Now under the command of Sqn Ldr C. W. Pearce, the squadron was moved to Mount Batten, where it was destined to remain for the rest of the war. 10 Squadron RAAF would become the first 'Dominion' squadron to operate in Europe during the war and the only such squadron to operate solidly from 1940 to 1945 in the European theatre. Yet another first for the Australian squadron was the award of the DFC to Sqn Ldr Pearce in July 1940, the unit's first decoration and the first DFC awarded to any member of the RAAF since it was formed.

Sunderland Mk I L2163 of 210 Squadron keeps a close eye on Canadian Troop Convoy 6 (T.C.6) in 1941, bound for Greenock. (Via Martyn Chorlton)

The SS *Kensington Court*

The war against the U-boat continued from the outset to the last day of the war, and, at first, the Sunderland was powerless to do anything about the threat because of a lack of appropriate anti-submarine weaponry. This would change, but during the early stages of the war, the requirement of all Coastal Command crews was to fly general reconnaissance and convoy escort protection from the air and sea, both above and below. While nothing could be done to stop the attack on SS *Kensington Court* on 18 September 1939, the support given by the Sunderland was a good example of air-sea co-operation.

The *Kensington Court* was a 4,900-ton merchant ship loaded with wheat, which it was transporting from Argentina to Birkenhead. While 70 miles off the Scillies, the ship was attacked by the surfaced U-32 forcing the ship's captain, J. Schofield, to order abandon ship.[2] An SOS signal was transmitted before the 34 crew members took to the ship's two lifeboats; the U-boat continued shelling until it was satisfied that *Kensington Court* was sinking. U-32 then left the scene, leaving the entire merchant ship's crew aboard a single lifeboat after the other became swamped.

The SOS was, fortunately, picked up by several Sunderlands that were operating within 100 miles of the incident. The first to arrive was 228 Squadron's N9025, flown by Flt Lt T. M. W. Smith, who landed within half a mile of the lifeboat. At once, the Sunderland's dinghies were launched using trailing lines and the sailors were quickly retrieved a few at a time. Not long after, a second Sunderland, L5802 of 204 Squadron flown by Flt Lt J. Barrett, also landed close to the scene. By now, Smith had 20 sailors on board leaving the remaining 14 for Barrett's aircraft. Within an hour of the *Kensington Court* being sunk, the entire crew were safely back in England. Both Barrett and Smith were later awarded the DFC at Buckingham Palace on 2 November. These were the first DFCs to be awarded to Sunderland aircrew.

---

2 U-32 was sunk on 20 October 1940 by a pair of Royal Navy destroyers.

The crew of the SS *Kensington Court* being rescued by Flt Lt T. M. W. Smith on 18 September 1939. (Via Owen Cooper)

Clearly, as depicted by this 1939 cartoon, the Sunderland was more than capable of carrying out a large-scale rescue at sea! (Via Owen Cooper)

Norway

It was on 30 January 1940 that the very first U-boat kill, U-55, was credited to 228 Squadron Sunderland Mk I N9025, flown by Fg Off E. J. Brooks. Admittedly, it was a shared kill with the Royal Navy, but nevertheless it was a start. By June, the enemy submarine tally began to rise, with Fg Off W. W. Campbell of 230 Squadron claiming two Italian submarines sunk on consecutive days in June 1940.

The same month, the Norwegian campaign reached a head and, in the lead up to the British Expeditionary Force (BEF) being evicted from the country, Sunderlands had played an important role. Several senior members of the Allied Forces in Norway were conveyed and later evacuated from the country, including the commander Maj Gen Paget and Carton de Wiart. Sunderlands saw a great deal of action along the Norwegian coast from December 1939 through to June 1940, including the infamous encounter with six Ju 88s experienced by the crew of N9046 on 3 April. Reconnaissance operations in support of the Home Fleet were carried out on a daily basis from April onwards, and several Sunderlands were lost without trace as a result; it later transpired that virtually all had been shot down by German aircraft.

Whilst searching for another Sunderland that went missing on 8 April, Wg Cdr Davis, 204 Squadron's OC, in Mk I N9844 encountered two enemy aircraft near Trondheim Fjord. The first was an Arado Ar 196 seaplane that tried to get on the tail of the big flying boat. At a range of 200 yards, the rear gunner opened fire but was halted when his rear escape door opened, temporarily jamming the turret. Davis pulled the Sunderland into a tight climbing turn that brought the front turret to bear on the Arado but the gunner missed his chance and did not open fire. The Arado then thought better of it before a second enemy aircraft, a Blohm & Voss seaplane, attacked from the rear. The Sunderland's rear turret was put out of action for a second time and the flying boat suffered several machine gun and cannon holes, some to its two inner fuel tanks. Return fire caused black smoke to pour from the enemy seaplane's port engine, which then also decided it had had enough. One of the Sunderland's crew, Flt Lt Hyde, climbed into the aircraft's wings and managed to block the holes in the fuel tanks with Plasticine. N9844 made it back to Sullom Voe with little difficulty, having also spotted the cruiser *Admiral Hipper* anchored near the entrance to Trondheim Fjord.

June 1940 also saw 228 Squadron begin operating against Italian shipping after the country had decided to enter the war on the side of the Axis powers. It was a 228 Squadron Sunderland, operating from Malta, which carried out the crucial reconnaissance operation over Taranto only days before the Fleet Air Arm made its successful Swordfish attack on the Italian fleet.

Mk II W3989 'L' of 228 Squadron on patrol over the Mediterranean in late 1941. (Via Martyn Chorlton)

The Sunderland was just as vulnerable as any other big aircraft during the early part of war. Whilst being flown by Flt Lt S. R. W. Hughes, T9071 of 230 Squadron was shot down by a pair of Bf 110s of III/ZG26 near Ras Amr, Libya, on 21 December 1941. (Via Owen Cooper)

View of Pembroke Dock in May 1943 with 228 Squadron and 461 Squadron RAAF in residence. (Via Owen Cooper)

Evacuation

The Sunderland earned a great deal of respect for its convoy escort and anti-submarine operations over the Atlantic, Indian Ocean, North Sea and Mediterranean, but its exploits when carrying out rescue and evacuations are legendary. One 'evacuation' that stands out above the rest took place off Crete on 25 April 1941. Flt Lt H. Lamond, flying 228 Squadron Sunderland Mk I T9048 'N', was ordered to fly to Githeon to 'lift' an RAF party waiting there. Following signals from a handmade mirror being sent from the shoreline, Lamond found the 'party', which numbered 101 officers and airmen of 112 Squadron under the command of Flt Lt Magner. Overloaded by 9,000lb, Lamond took 52 airmen on board and flew them to Suda, having promised those who remained on Crete that he would return that evening. Instead, Lamond was ordered to fly to Kalamata to evacuate both army and RAF personnel. With little fuel on board, Lamond calculated that he could carry 80 of them although 82 were counted once in the air. Including the crew, T9048 had 92 people on board, a clear unbeaten record for a Sunderland. Lamond later reported, '… it was no trouble to T9048 and she took off like a bird'.

By late 1941, the Sunderland Mk I began to make way for the Mk II, which first flew in August. The Mk II was fitted with a twin-gun power-operated dorsal turret instead of the open hatch beam gun – a feature that would also become standard on the most prolific variant produced, the Sunderland Mk III. The first production aircraft, W3999, took off from the River Medway on 15 December 1941. The Mk III differed mainly from its predecessors in the redesigned planing bottom of its hull, which had a shallower forward step. This made the aircraft much easier to handle on the water. Both Mk IIs and MK IIIs were powered by the 1,065hp Pegasus XVIII engines, a powerplant that would remain with the Sunderlands until the introduction of the Mk V in February 1945. This final military variant of the flying boat was powered by four Pratt & Whitney Twin Wasp engines, and, in this guise, the Sunderland would see out its days with the RAF.

More firepower

By early 1943, Coastal Command had nine operational Sunderland squadrons, two of which operated with the RAAF: 10 and 461 squadrons. It was crews of the former who came up with the idea of giving the Sunderland more firepower, especially while tackling a heavily armed U-boat. By 1943, U-boats were choosing to slug it out on the surface and the majority were now armed with 37mm and 20mm anti-aircraft guns, both capable of bringing a slow-flying Sunderland down into the sea. To counter the German deck gunners, four .303in machine guns (two each side) were fitted into the nose of the flying boat and this, combined with the guns in the front turret, gave the Sunderland good forward firepower. The guns were shown off to good effect on 8 January 1944, when Sunderland Mk III EK586 of 10 Squadron RAAF opened fire on U-426 at 1,200 yards. All enemy gunners were killed, and the U-Boat was sunk on a single pass.

The Australians achieved yet another Sunderland 'first' on 29 May 1943. The previous day, Flt Lt W. S. E. Dods of 461 Squadron set off from Pembroke Dock looking for the crew of a Whitley that was forced to ditch in the Bay of Biscay. After receiving permission to land, Dods' Sunderland bounced three times on the heavy sea before the forward fuselage snapped to the rear of the cockpit, killing the pilot instantly. The rest of the crew survived and, after climbing into their own dinghy, joined up with the Whitley crew. Another 461 Squadron aircraft, Sunderland Mk II T9114 with Plt Off G. O. Singleton at the controls, was soon on its way to the scene. After landing next to the stranded crews and taking them on board, the Sunderland was too heavy to take off in the rough sea. The *La Combattante*, a French sloop, was contacted and, after transferring the ditched crews, the Sunderland was taken under tow with just essential crew on board. Over four and a half hours later, the tow rope broke, and, with little choice, Singleton started T9114's engines. It took a take-off run of more than three miles before the Sunderland was released from the heavy sea, by which time the hull had a 7ft-long gash in it. Singleton now faced a dilemma: land on the sea at base and risk the lives of his remaining crew or try and land on an airfield. The latter was wisely chosen, and Singleton executed a perfect approach and landing at Angle, Pembrokeshire, coming to a halt in just a few hundred yards alongside the main runway. This was the first time such a feat had been carried out, and many flying boats have been landed on dry land since with little further damage being caused.

It was another 461 Squadron Sunderland involved in an epic battle that saw the level of defensive armament raised. On 2 June 1943, Flt Lt G. P. Weatherlake in Sunderland Mk III EJ134 was carrying out a convoy escort patrol over the Bay of Biscay when the flying boat came under attack by eight Ju 88s. Incredibly, EJ134 survived the ordeal and even managed to shoot down three of the Junkers before returning to Pembroke Dock with over 200 cannon and machine gun holes. Unsurprisingly, the Sunderland was written off. As a result of this encounter with the enemy and several others over the Bay of Biscay, the Sunderland's defensive armament was increased with a pair of 0.5in guns fitted in the galley position. The heavier American-made guns were retrofitted to the majority of serving Sunderlands and were retained until the type retired.

Above left: 10 Squadron RAAF Sunderland 'Z' taxies out of the Cattewater at Mount Batten in 1942. (Via Martyn Chorlton)

Above right: Mk III ML830 'A' of 10 Squadron RAAF being hauled up the slipway at Mount Batten in late 1944. (Via Owen Cooper)

Anti-Submarine

By 1944, it was the anti-submarine war that dominated Sunderland operations and, although a comparative handful of U-boats were actually sunk by the flying boat, an untold number were kept under the surface, away from their intended targets. The invasion of Europe saw the U-boat's operating area begin to shrink and successes begin to increase.

From January to April 1945, 16 Sunderlands were lost in accidents or written off because of the weather – none due to enemy action. During this same period, Sunderland crews also claimed 30 U-boats sunk, but in reality, none were lost or even damaged, despite their best efforts.

When the war finally came to an end on 8 May 1945, Coastal Command continued to hunt for U-boats and those not flying the black 'surrender' flag were susceptible to being attacked. The submarine patrols continued until 3–4 June, when Wg Cdr J. Barrett DFC, flying Sunderland Mk III ML778 of 228 Squadron, received a 'cease' order while airborne on a convoy escort patrol. This was the last official wartime patrol of Coastal Command, giving the Sunderland the honour of flying the war's first and last operational sortie.

The end of the war in Europe saw six of the seven UK-based Sunderland squadrons either transferred or disbanded within a few months. 10 Squadron RAAF, 228 Squadron, 422 and 423 RCAF Squadrons and 461 Squadron RAAF were disbanded before the end of 1945, while 330 Squadron was transferred to the Norwegian Air Force. Only 201 Squadron survived the post-war cuts, continuing as a Sunderland unit until 1957. Further afield, 95, 204 and 270 squadrons and 490 RNZAF Squadron were disbanded in 1945, while 343 Squadron lived on with the Aeronavale. 95, 204 and 270 squadrons suffered the humiliation of having to destroy their own trusty Sunderlands by scuttling them.

The Sunderland served the RAF with distinction throughout World War Two and, despite the seemingly unnecessary way that many were disposed of, the type, unlike many others that saw wartime service, would live on into the post-war years.

A U-boat displays the black 'surrender' flag as viewed from a 228 Squadron Sunderland. (Via Owen Cooper)

'Z for Zebra' makes its last patrol. Captained by Wg Cdr J. Barrett DSO and manned by a British, Dominions and Colonial crew from a squadron of RAF Coastal Command, 'Z for Zebra', a Sunderland V flying boat, carried out Coastal Command's last convoy escort for the Royal Navy. At 0001hrs on 4 June 1945, when patrolling, a convoy received the 'cease patrol' order and thanks. (British Official caption and photograph No. CH15303 via Martyn Chorlton)

Chapter 5

The Sunderland and the Fight Against the Submarine

U-boats damaged by Sunderlands

U-55 – 30 January 1940

The first U-boat sinking credited to a Sunderland was a good example of co-operation between the RAF, the Royal Navy and the French Navy.

U-55 was on its very first patrol under the command of Werner Heidel when it put to sea from Kiel on 16 January 1940. Only two days later, the crew tasted success when 1,304-ton SS *Foxen* was sunk, and, on 30 January, Heidel could not believe his luck when he intercepted a convoy southwest of the Isles of Scilly. In short order, the U-boat had despatched 5,026-ton MV *Vaclite* and 5,085-ton SS *Keramiai*, but the commotion the attack caused alerted a host of Allied forces in the area.

First on the scene was British sloop HMS *Fowey*, joined by 228 Squadron Sunderland Mk II N9025 with Fg Off E. J. Brooks at the controls. The combined depth charge attack forced U-55 to the surface, by which time destroyer HMS *Whitshed* and French destroyers *Valmy* and *Guépard* had also joined the fight. While Brooks stood off, the Allied ships' firepower forced Heidel to scuttle U-55, from which 41 survivors were rescued. Werner Heidel was the only casualty, choosing to go down with his vessel.

U-26 – 1 July 1940

U-26 was already a veteran of five war patrols and had a tally of seven ships sunk, totalling 33,153 tons. On 20 June 1940, U-26, under the command of Heinz Scheringer, left its home base of Wilhemshaven for the final time. Nine days later, U-26 sunk 6,701-ton SS *Frangoula Goulandris* 200 miles off the southern coast of Ireland. On 30 June, the *Belmoira* and *Merkur* were also sunk, with the seemingly unstoppable U-26 going on to intercept convoy OA-175 south-southwest of Ireland that evening.

Only corvette HMS *Gladiolus* was on hand to protect the convoy, which spotted the U-boat on the surface before it continued to stalk the vessels under the waves. *Gladiolus* investigated the reported sighting, but it was not until 0118hrs on 1 July that U-26 appeared again, after torpedoing 4,871-ton SS *Zarian*. *Gladiolus* returned to the convoy immediately and when the U-boat spotted the corvette, it was forced to crash-dive. The corvette attacked U-26 four times, unknowingly causing sufficient damage to immobilise the U-boat under the surface. Six hours later, U-26 was forced to surface just 800 yards from the unsuspecting *Gladiolus* and succeeding in escaping onto the surface.

At 0815hrs, however, U-26's luck ran out when the boat was spotted by 10 Squadron RAAF Sunderland Mk I P9603 being flown by Flt Lt W. M. 'Hoot' Gibson DFC. On sighting the approaching Sunderland, Scheringer attempted to crash-dive again, but the four 250lb Anti-Submarine (A/S) bombs dropped forced U-26 to the surface again. Gibson made a second pass, dropping another quartet of A/S bombs, which exploded just over 100ft from the enemy boat. By now, HMS *Gladiolus* had spotted the action but was outpaced to the scene by sloop HMS *Rochester*, which had been escorting a second convoy nearby. U-26 was incapable of diving, and the crew prepared to abandon and scuttle the U-boat, despite the attempts by the *Rochester* to stop them. All 48 crew on board survived the ordeal to be rescued by the *Rochester*, while their boat sank stern first in the open Atlantic.

U-465 – 2 May 1943

On 29 April 1943, U-465 slipped out of St Nazaire under the command of Heinz Wolf, who was hoping to score his first victory since the boat began operations in May 1942. The U-boat had already had encounters with enemy aircraft, firstly in February 1943 when it was damaged by a 120 Squadron Liberator and again in April by a Catalina of 210 Squadron. Little did Wolf know that his own fate, and that of his crew, would be sealed from the air.

During the early hours of 2 May, 461 Squadron RAAF Sunderland Mk III DV968, flown by Flt Lt E. C. Smith DFC, took off from Pembroke Dock, bound for a long patrol over the Bay of Biscay. After several hours in the air, a U-boat was spotted 110 miles north of Cape Finisterre, Spain, and, without hesitation, Smith attacked U-465 with A/S bombs, despatching the U-boat in a single pass. Although approximately 15 sailors were seen to escape the crippled boat, none were rescued and all 48 crew perished.

After well over three and a half years of trying, Smith and his crew had become the first airmen to sink a U-boat, unaided, with a Sunderland.

U-663 – 7 May 1943

It was while carrying out another long-range patrol on 7 May 1943 that the crew of a 10 Squadron RAAF Sunderland spotted the tell-tale signs of a U-boat just under the surface. The boat in question was U-663, which had been at sea since March and was most likely returning to Brest. It is not clear how many times the Sunderland attacked or how many depth charges were dropped, but the result was a severely damaged U-663. What is known is that the attack was serious enough for the U-boat to survive only another 24 hours before it sank nearly 300 miles from Brest, with the loss of all 49 on board.

U-753 – 13 May 1943

By mid-1943, the experience levels of the U-boat commanders were at their peak, and Alfred Mannhardt von Mannstein, the commander of U-753, was no exception. He had been in charge of U-753 since its first patrol from Kiel in January 1942 and, on 5 May 1943, had just departed La Pallice on the boat's sixth.

The action took place far out in the Atlantic, almost 600 miles off the southwest coast of Ireland, 500 miles northeast of the Azores on 13 May 1943. The demise of U-753 was once again a combined effort with frigate HMS *Lagan*, Canadian corvette HMCS *Drumheller* and 423 Squadron RCAF Sunderland Mk III W6006 taking part. U-753 was spotted while trying to attack convoy HX.237, but before Mannstein had a chance to fire a single torpedo, a well-co-ordinated depth charge attack was orchestrated between the Allied warships and the Sunderland, sinking the U-boat instantly with the loss of all 47 hands.

U-440 – 31 May 1943

U-440 was another U-boat that had not sunk a single enemy ship despite carrying out four war patrols since September 1942. On its fifth patrol, the boat gained a new commander, Werner Schwaff, and the crew had high hopes that their luck would finally change. Unfortunately for them, it was not to be and, just five days after leaving St Nazaire, the U-boat was spotted northwest of Cape Ortegal, Spain, by 201 Squadron Sunderland Mk III DD835 'R' out of Lough Erne. Flt Lt D. M. Gall DFC and crew attacked with four depth charges and sank the U-boat with the loss of all 46 hands.

U-563 – 31 May 1943

Gustav Borchardt's U-563 was in the wrong place at the wrong time on 31 May 1943, when it was attacked by a Halifax and two Sunderlands, 290 miles west-southwest of Brest. The U-boat stood no chance as 58 Squadron Halifax HR477, 10 Squadron RAAF Sunderland Mk III DV969, flown by Flt Lt M. S. Mainprize DFC, and 228 Squadron Sunderland Mk III DD838, flown by Fg Off W. M. French DFC, attacked it. Immediately after U-563 sank, at least 30 survivors were seen in the water wearing life jackets, but, sadly, no rescue was forthcoming, and 49 crewmen lost their lives.

U-607 – 13 July 1943

Commissioned in January 1942, by May 1943, U-607 had sunk four ships totalling 28,937 tons and damaged two more, adding another 15,201 tons to its war tally so far. Under the command of Wolf Jeschonnek, the U-boat set sail from St Nazaire on its fifth war patrol on 10 July 1943 with the task of laying mines off Jamaica.

However, U-607 was not bargaining on the keen eyes of the crew of 228 Squadron Sunderland Mk III JM708 being flown by Fg Off R. D. Hanbury DOS, DFC. Just before 0800hrs on 13 July, Hanbury attacked the U-boat northwest of Cape Ortegal with depth charges. U-607 had no chance and it was quickly abandoned by its 52 crew, of whom at least 25 were seen in the water. HMS *Wren* was nearby but could only manage to rescue seven of the crew by the time it got to the scene.

U-461 – 30 July 1943

The defeat the U-boat fleet suffered at the hands of Coastal Command on 30 July 1943 forced the enemy to restrict the number of boats it was sending across the Bay of Biscay. There were three U-boats: two of them, U-461 and U-462, were Type XIV 'Milk Cow' tankers, in company with U-504, a Type XIV/40, all leaving Bordeaux on 27 July. Just three days later, they were spotted on the surface by a 53 Squadron Liberator northwest of Cape Ortegal, which loitered out of range while further aircraft and Royal Navy ships were called into the area.

Within a short period of time, the Liberator was joined by a pair of Halifaxes from 502 Squadron, a Catalina from 210 Squadron, 228 Squadron Sunderland Mk III JM679 and 461 Squadron RAAF Sunderland Mk III W6077, flown by Flt Lt D. Marrows DSO and crew. The ensuing battle, at first, went the U-boat's way as one Halifax was seriously damaged by flak and the 53 Squadron Liberator had two engines shot out after its depth charges fell short of the target. The Liberator made for Spain but managed to turn south for Portugal where the crew were interned.

While the action was taking place, Flt Lt Marrows placed his Sunderland behind the attacking Liberator and dropped four A/S bombs close to U-461. The damage caused was sufficient to force the crew to abandon the U-boat, but out of the 68 on board, only 15 survived. By the end of the action, U-462 was sunk by a Halifax and U-504 was depth charged and eventually sunk by the Royal Navy.

The day had been a disaster for the Germans and the loss of two 'Milk Cows' in a single action (there were only ten Type XIVs built) virtually brought long-distance operations to an end. Sailing U-boats in groups across the Bay of Biscay was stopped, as it was clear by now that the Royal Navy and Coastal Command had finally gained the upper hand.

U-454 – 1 August 1943

Electing to stay on the surface and slug it out with an attacking aircraft was always an option for a U-boat commander and, up to 1 August 1943, this was encouraged by Karl Dönitz, Befehlshaber der U-Boote (BdU, Commander of U-boats).

U-454 had been under the command of Burckhard Hackländer since it was commissioned on 24 July 1940. The U-boat had only sunk two ships, totalling 2,427 tons, spread over nine war patrols, and its record gave the impression that its activities were all about surviving and not sinking enemy ships.

At 1440hrs on 1 August 1943, Hackländer's luck appeared to have run out. His U-boat was spotted on the surface, northwest of Cape Ortegal by 10 Squadron RAAF Sunderland Mk III W4020, being flown by Fg Off K. G. Fry. Fry did not hesitate to attack and, unbeknown to him, Hackländer had no choice but to stay on the surface because his batteries were low after spending a long time under the water.

As Fry closed on U-454, the U-boat's flak gunners retaliated, and shells poured into the flying boat. Before depth charges could be released, the Sunderland's front gunner, Sgt J. E. Fryer (actually a fitter) was shot dead and Fry, his co-pilot, the second navigator and flight engineer were wounded, several of them mortally. The charges were dropped as the Sunderland swooped over the U-boat, which was lifted out of the water by the blast and broken in two. By this stage, the Sunderland was in an equally critical condition, with fuel pouring out of its holed tanks. Fry, who was seriously injured, managed to retain control long enough to ditch his aircraft into the Atlantic. The giant flying boat nosed into the sea and water gushed in at an alarming rate. Luckily, the Royal Navy was on the scene very quickly, but out of the 12-man Sunderland crew, only six were rescued by HMS *Wren* from 2nd Escort Group. Meanwhile, a large number of U-454's crew were also in the water and 14 were picked out by HMS *Kite* including the boat's captain, Hackländer, who survived the war as a POW. Thirty-two of his crew did not.

U-383 – 1 August 1943

Later the same day, another Sunderland crew from 228 Squadron spotted a U-boat on the surface in the Bay of Biscay only a few days out of Brest. The target, U-383, under the command of Horst Kremser, had shot down an unknown Allied aircraft a few days earlier.

At 2002hrs, the pilot of Sunderland Mk III JM678, Flt Lt S. White DFC, commenced his attack run, strafing U-383 from bow to stern as they closed in. The defending fire from the U-boat was accurate; the Sunderland's starboard float and aileron were shot away and the fuselage was holed in several places. The damage caused to the Sunderland and the vigorous evasive action carried out by U-383 ensured that White's first attack failed to make its mark. However, undeterred, White went round for a second pass and, after dropping a stick of seven depth charges, the U-boat was left listing heavily to port and several crew were spotted jumping into the water. White wisely headed back to Pembroke Dock, rather than risk soaking up more damage from the stricken U-boat.

U-383 clung on for several more hours and managed to send at least one distress signal to BdU HQ. Three German torpedo boats responded, but by the time they got to the area of U-383's last transmission, the U-boat had gone, along with all 52 hands.

U-106 – 2 August 1943

It had been a lean time for U-106, which, up to October 1942 had sunk 22 ships totalling 138,581 tons and damaged four others including battleship HMS *Malaya*. Since then, prey had been scarce despite a war patrol along the US coast during February and March 1943. On 28 July, U-106 was back at sea, departing from Lorient, crossing the Bay of Biscay into the open Atlantic on its tenth and final war patrol.

The outbound journey had already been challenging and, on 1 August, a determined 407 Squadron RCAF crew in their Wellington dropped six depth charges on U-106 and continued to shadow the U-boat until more Allied forces were called in. From this point, there was really no hope for a sighted U-boat and, on 2 August, a pair of Sunderlands joined the fray. It was a combined depth charge attack by 228 Squadron Sunderland Mk III JM708 flown by Fg Off Hanbury DSO and 461 Squadron Sunderland DV698, being piloted by Flt Lt I. Clarke DFC, that sealed U-106's fate. The only saving grace for the U-boat crew was that the German torpedo-boats T22, T24 and T25 were already in the area looking for survivors from U-383. Twenty-two crew were killed but 36 were very lucky to be rescued, including the boat's commander Wolf-Dietrich Damerow.

U-489 – 4 August 1943
An epic battle between a Sunderland and a U-boat that produced no winners – both the Type XIV 'Milk Cow' and the attacking 423 Squadron RCAF Sunderland were lost in the action. The full story of the demise of U-489 is covered in detail in the next chapter.

U-610 – 8 October 1943
A classic example of a Sunderland protecting a convoy was illustrated by Fg Off A. H. Russell DFC and his 423 Squadron RCAF crew on 8 October 1943. Their aircraft was Sunderland Mk III DD863 and, whilst keeping a close eye on Convoy SC.143, 480 miles south-southwest of Iceland, U-610 was spotted preparing to attack. Decisive action saw the Sunderland carry out a single attack run and, after several depth charges were dropped, the U-boat descended to the depths taking 51 crew members with it.

U-426 – 8 January 1944
It was destined to be a short career for U-426, a Type VIIC U-boat, which only carried out its first patrol during November and December 1943. With a single 6,625-ton ship to its credit, U-426 under the command of Christian Reich set sail from Brest on 3 January 1944. Five days later, the U-boat was spotted by 10 Squadron RAAF Sunderland Mk III EK586, 230 miles north of Cape Ortegal. Little detail is known of the attack, but the Australian-manned Sunderland made short work of the U-boat, which was abandoned after a single attacking pass. Over 40 men were spotted in the sea but unfortunately, their fate was sealed as all 51 hands were lost.

U-571 – 28 January 1944
Up to April 1943, U-571 had been enjoying a fruitful career, which, by this stage, was made up of seven ships sunk, totalling 47,169 tons over ten war patrols since August 1941. However, for the next nine months, U-571 had seen no action, other than being attacked by a 26 Squadron South African Air Force (SAAF) Wellington operating from Takoradi, West Africa, on 22 July 1943.

U-571's demise would ultimately come from the air, when it was attacked again on 28 January 1944 by 10 Squadron RAAF Sunderland Mk III EK575 flown by Flt Lt R. D. Lucas DFC. Details are sketchy but the action took place 180 miles west of Ireland. A single depth charge attack sent U-571 to the bottom of the Atlantic with 52 crew on board.

U-625 – 10 March 1944
Commissioned in June 1942, U-625 was a Type VIIC boat initially under the command of Hans Benker. Benker met his end during an air attack by a pair of 224 Squadron Liberators from St Eval on 2 January 1944. The order to crash-dive was given whilst the bridge party, including Benker, were left topside. Despite surfacing to look for the missing crew a few minutes later, Benker was never found, although one other seaman was lucky to be rescued.

A few days later, U-625 returned to Brest for repairs, only to leave again on 29 February 1944 on its tenth war patrol. After reaching its designated patrol area, 380 miles off the west coast of Ireland, the U-boat was spotted by Flt Lt S. W. Butler DFC and his 422 Squadron RCAF crew in Sunderland Mk III EK591. The U-boat was quickly despatched by depth charges, followed by a high proportion of the crew abandoning the vessel. Unfortunately, all 53 hands were to perish that evening in a violent storm.

U-675 – 24 May 1944

U-675 had only been commissioned on 14 July 1943 and, under the command of Karl-Heinz Sammler, set out on its first war patrol from Kristiansand on 18 May 1944. After several days at sea, the U-boat was spotted by 4 OTU Sunderland Mk III ML736 flown by Fg Off T. F. P. Frizell DFC, on a long-range exercise, as part of the crew's final stage of operational training.

U-675 was sighted 100 miles west of Ålesund and was attacked accurately with depth charges. U-675 sank quickly, taking all 51 hands with it.

U-955 – 7 June 1944

Another U-boat that contributed very little to the BdU effort was U-995, which had set out on its first war patrol on 1 April 1944. It was while making its return en route to Bergen, Norway, that the U-boat was spotted by a 201 Squadron Sunderland from Pembroke Dock. The experienced Flt Lt L. H. Baveystock DSO, DFC, DFM and his crew in Sunderland Mk III 'S' made short work of the U-boat with a stick of depth charges. The boat went down 100 miles north of Carino, Spain, in the Canatabria Knoll area, with the loss of all 50 hands.

U-970 – 7 June 1944

With no enemy shipping to its credit, U-970, under the command of Hans-Heinrich Ketels, embarked from La Pallice on 6 June 1944 on its second and final war patrol. In less than 24 hours, the U-boat was spotted 175 miles west of Bordeaux by 228 Squadron Sunderland Mk III ML877, flown by Flt Lt C. G. D. Lancaster and crew. Thirty-eight hands were lost in the attack, although 14 crew did survive, but their rescuer is unknown.

U-243 – 8 July 1944

Another U-boat that had a short operational career was U-243, a Type VIIC that was commissioned on 2 October 1943. Under the command of Hans Märtens, the boat did not set sail until early June 1944 when it moved from Flekkefj to Bergen, before setting out on its first war patrol on 15 June. It was while beginning the return journey of this patrol that the U-boat was spotted on 8 July, by 10 Squadron RAAF Sunderland Mk III W4030, 230 miles west of Nantes. Fg Off W. B. Tilley DFC and crew attacked U-243 successfully with depth charges, forcing the crew to abandon the boat. HMCS *Restigouche* rescued 38 crew, including Märtens; however, the commander later died of head injuries.

U-1222 – 11 July 1944

U-1222 was also on its first war patrol when it left Kiel on 13 April 1944, under the command of the experienced Heinz Bielfeld. A lengthy operation conducted along the Canadian coast bore no fruit and, in late June, U-1222 began the long journey back across the Atlantic. The boat was destined never to make it home. When U-1222 was just under 200 miles from La Rochelle, it was spotted by a 201 Squadron Sunderland from Pembroke Dock. The aircraft, Sunderland Mk III ML881, flown by Flt Lt I. B. F. Walters DFC and Bar,[3] sunk U-1222 with depth charges, resulting in the loss of all 56 hands.

U-385 – 11 August 1944

With just one unsuccessful war patrol under his belt, Hans-Guido Valentiner hoped to change that upon leaving St Nazaire on 9 August 1944. Unfortunately, only two days later, U-385 was attacked and damaged by 461 Squadron RAAF Sunderland Mk III ML741, flown by Plt Off I. F. Southall DFC.

---

3   Walters was awarded two bars to his DFC.

U-385 survived this initial attack but was forced to the surface by depth charges dropped by HMS *Starling* and then sunk by gunfire. All but one of the crew managed to escape the sinking U-boat.

U-270 – 13 August 1944

Commissioned in September 1942, U-270 departed Kiel in March 1943 and from then on operated from St Nazaire. Five war patrols were carried out up to January 1944, but only a single ship, 1,370-ton frigate HMS *Lagan*, had been sunk. Despite this, the U-boat had seen a great deal of action, much of it from the air, and U-270 also had a 53 Squadron Liberator and a 206 Squadron Fortress to its credit.

On 10 August 1944, U-270 was tasked with evacuating German personnel from La Pallice, which it duly did two days later. Unfortunately, the boat was caught on the surface 65 miles west of La Rochelle on 13 August by 461 Squadron RAAF Sunderland Mk III ML735, flown by Fg Off D. A. Little DFC. U-270 was bombed and sunk by depth charges; 71 on board were rescued, while ten perished.

U-107 – 18 August 1944

Unbeknown to the crew of a 201 Squadron Sunderland Mk III, the U-boat they attacked and sunk on 18 August 1944 was the most successful in the BdU. Back in 1941 and under the command of Günter Hessler, and only on its second war patrol, U-107 tallied 14 ships totalling 86,699 tons – a record by a considerable margin for a single patrol. By the time the boat set sail on its thirteenth and final war patrol from Lorient on 16 August 1944, U-107 had sunk 39 ships, which equated to 217,786 tons, plus another four ships damaged.

U-107's luck ran out just two days after leaving port, when Sunderland Mk III EJ150, being flown by Flt Lt Baveystock DSO, DFM, DFM brought the boat's record to an end 110 miles west of La Rochelle. All 58 hands perished.

U-297 – 6 December 1944

The demise of U-297 is a little confusing because some sources credit a pair of frigates, HMS *Goodall* and *Loch Irish* with the kill, while others credit a 201 Squadron Sunderland. It is most likely that both attacks brought about the loss, which took place 16 miles west of Yesnaby on the Orkney Islands. All 50 on board were lost.

U-51 – 16 August 1940

Having escaped an attack by French submarine *Orphée* in April, U-51 was lucky to escape the depth charges of Fg Off Baker's 210 Squadron Sunderland on 16 August 1940. The attack took place 350 miles off Corunna, Spain, while the U-boat was shadowing convoy OA-198. It is not clear what condition the Sunderland left U-51 in, but just four days later, the U-boat was destroyed by a single torpedo from HMS *Cachalot*.

U-568 – 9 January 1942

Under the command of KptLt Joachim Preuss since it was commissioned on 1 May 1941, U-568 had been serving with 29 Flottille in the Mediterranean since 1 January 1942. Just eight days later, the U-boat was sighted 50 miles off the Egyptian coast by Sqn Ldr Garside and crew in their 230 Squadron Sunderland. Three depth charges and four 250lb A/S bombs were dropped, convincing Garside that he had actually sunk U-577 (sunk by Swordfish six days later). U-568 managed to escape with minor damage, only to be sunk by the combined attack of HMS *Eridge*, *Hero* and *Hurworth* off Tobruk on 29 May 1942.

U-71 – 5 June 1942

It was an eventful patrol for the crew of 10 Squadron RAAF Sunderland Mk II W3986 on 5 June 1942. Flown by Flt Lt S. R. C. Wood, the crew spotted U-71 on the surface, 200 miles from La Pallice at 1549hrs. Wood attacked with eight depth charges set to a shallow depth, followed by a second pass when the U-boat was strafed with over 2,000 rounds of ammunition. The commander, KrvKpt Walter Flachsenberg managed to crash-dive U-71 from further danger and had no choice but to return to port. Wood continued to circle the spot where the U-boat went down until, two hours later, an Fw 200 Condor from I./Kg 40 attacked the Sunderland. In the lengthy exchange of fire that followed, both aircraft were damaged and two airmen on the Sunderland were injured, forcing Wood to set course for home.

U-105 – 11 June 1942

It was the turn of Flt Lt Martin and his 10 Squadron RAAF crew in Sunderland Mk II W3993 to attack a U-boat on 11 June 1942. U-105 was caught on the surface whilst crossing the Bay of Biscay and was crash-diving as Martin released six depth charges and a pair of 250lb A/S bombs on the enemy boat.

   Seriously damaged, the U-boat made for El Ferrol, Spain, and remained there until 28 June when it left for Lorient. Arriving two days later, it did not leave again until 23 November, such was the extent of the damage.

U-608 – 19 March 1943

Although U-608 never reported being attacked on 19 March 1943, the crew of 228 Squadron Sunderland Mk III DD837 certainly thought they had, while escorting Convoy SC122/HX229. Flt Lt Church encountered the U-boat approximately 550 miles west of Ireland and attacked it with four depth charges, completely convinced that it had been damaged as a result.

U-526 – 20 March 1943

On 20 March 1943, U-526 had the same Convoy SC122/HX229 in its sights. Flt Lt Hewitt in his 201 Squadron Sunderland Mk III DD829 spotted the U-boat and dropped six depth charges, apparently causing the U-boat slight damage.

U-441 – 24 May 1943

It would have been some consolation to Fg Off H. J. Debnam and his ten-man crew to know that they seriously damaged the U-boat that took their lives on 24 May 1943. A combination of strafing and five depth charges dropped by Sunderland Mk III EJ139 at 2050hrs, during the aircraft's final moments, forced U-411 to return to base early.

U-564 – 13 June 1943

As with the previous entry, it took the sacrifice of an entire crew and their aircraft to damage U-564 on 13 June 1943. Fg Off L. B. Lee of 228 Squadron came across five outbound U-boats northwest of Cape Finisterre. Lee singled out U-564 but, after dropping depth charges and bombs, the Sunderland succumbed to a barrage of anti-aircraft fire and crashed in flames. U-564 was forced to return to base in company with U-185 and, early the next morning, managed to shoot down a 10 OTU Whitley, which was determined to sink one of the U-boats. However, U-564's luck ran out during the afternoon of 14 June, when another Whitley managed to cause enough damage to sink the U-boat.

U-518 – 27 June 1943
U-518 was outbound from the Lorient on 27 June 1943 when the U-boat was attacked by 201 Squadron Sunderland Mk III W6005, flown by Fg Off B. E. H. Layne of the RNZAF. Four depth charges were dropped on the U-boat at 1235hrs, west of Cape Finisterre, forcing U-518 to return to Bordeaux for repairs.

U-518 – 30 June 1943
Three days after the first air attack, Flt Lt H. W. Skinner and his 10 Squadron RAAF crew spotted U-518 making steady progress towards Bordeaux. Two attacking runs were made but all five depth charges overshot the target. Accurate defending fire from U-518's gunners fatally injured the rear gunner and punched several large holes in the Sunderland's wings.

U-119 – 29 April 1943
At 1124hrs a pair of 461 Squadron Sunderlands caught U-119 on the surface and, despite several depth charges being dropped, the U-boat escaped with little damage, although one crewman was killed on the deck by machine gun fire.

U-448 – 17 October 1943
This was another attack that came at great cost to the attacking Sunderland that instigated it, Mk III JM712 of 422 Squadron. At 1248hrs, Flt Lt P. T. Sargent engaged U-448 following a radar contact from Convoy ONS-20 located nearby. U-281 was also not far away and, during Sargent's first run, also opened fire, which was probably a contributory factor to the Sunderland dropping its first four depth charges short of the mark. As Sargent banked around for the second attack, the Sunderland's gunners fired at both U-boats and the big flying boat lined up for a second run. Two more depth charges were dropped, but the defending anti-aircraft fire was finding its mark, killing the front gunner outright and mortally wounding the navigator. JM712 was in such a state by now that Sargent was forced to ditch into the sea; the resulting crash killing the pilot and two more crew. Seven 422 Squadron aircrew were rescued by HMS *Drury*, while U-448 had to abort its patrol because of the damage caused by the last pair of depth charges.

U-672 – 24 April 1944
Flt Lt G. Fellows and his 423 Squadron crew were formally credited with sinking U-311 on 24 April 1944, but in fact had severely damaged U-672. Flt Lt Fellows made a single attack on the U-boat, 350 miles west of Ireland with six depth charges. Five landed close to the U-boat, but the sixth exploded prematurely, nearly bringing the Sunderland down. Fellows managed to bring the damaged Sunderland back home to Castle Archdale.

U-995 – 21 May 1944
Plt Off King was flying an 'armed' 4 OTU training sortie on 21 May 1944 when a U-boat was spotted on the surface 240 miles west of Trondheim. The boat was U-995 and the Sunderland made a single run, dropping six depth charges close to it. Five seamen on the U-boat were wounded but U-995 survived the attack and also the war, one of the few listed here to do so.

U-921 – 24 May 1944
It was while looking for U-476, which had already been seriously damaged by a Catalina, that 422 Squadron Sunderland Mk III DV990 flown by Fg Off G. E. Holley came across U-921. Holley

began his attack at 1420hrs, but the anti-aircraft fire from U-921 was so accurate that the Sunderland was shot out of the sky before the three depth charges, planned for the U-boat, came anywhere nearby. All 12 airmen on board were killed.

Only 12 miles distant, Flt Lt R. H. Nesbitt flying his 423 Squadron Sunderland Mk III DW111 had witnessed DV990 crashing into the sea. Nesbitt turned towards the scene and, with U-921 still on the surface, dropped five depth charges and strafed the deck of the U-boat. Three crewmen were wounded including the commander, Oblt Wolfgang Leu, who selflessly helped his two wounded comrades back into the U-boat. As the U-boat was crash-diving, rather than risk flooding U-921, he closed the hatch from the outside and drowned as a consequence.

U-333 – 10–11 June 1944
Possibly one of the luckiest U-boats at sea during World War Two, U-333 managed to escape with severe damage on 10 June 1944, when Flt Lt H. A. McGregor and crew in their 10 Squadron RAAF Sunderland attacked. The experienced deck gunners managed to repel the flying boat, but another would return the following day.

Flt Lt M. E. Slaughter and crew dropped further depth charges on U-333 but their 228 Squadron Sunderland was shot down into the sea, with the loss of all on board. U-333 managed to limp into La Pallice for repairs.

U-387 – 20 July 1944
Lt B. Thurmann-Nielson of 330 (Norwegian) Squadron was operating over familiar waters when U-387 was sighted on the surface 200 miles west of Bodø. Six depth charges were dropped on the U-boat, which aborted its patrol and headed to Narvik for repairs.

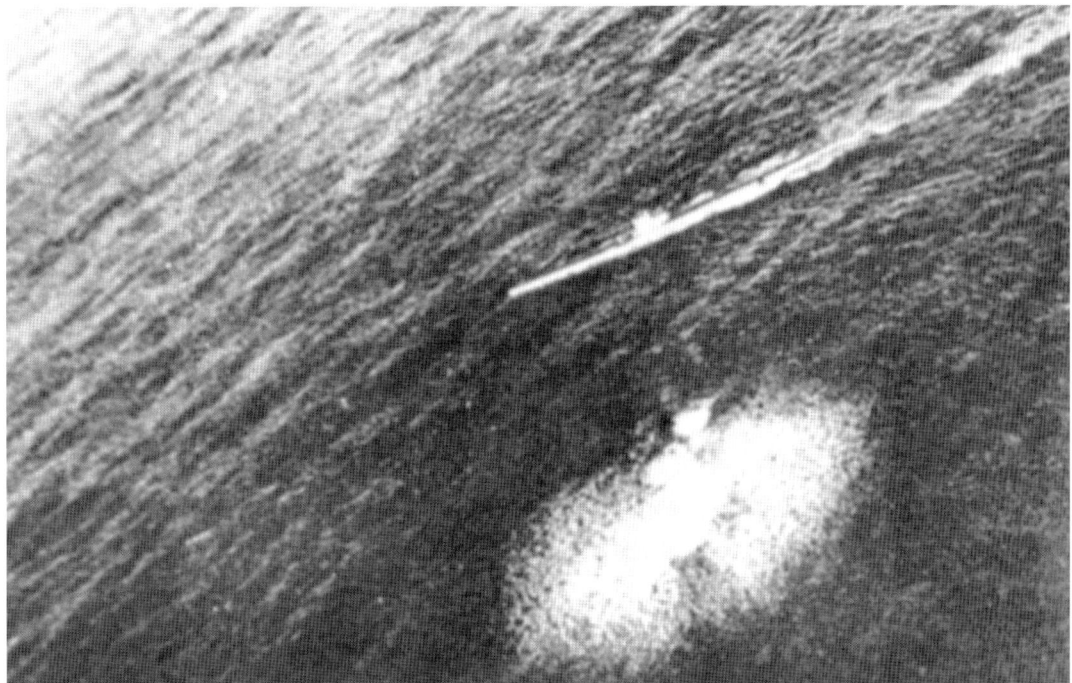

U-26 pictured during Flt Lt W. N. Gibson's second pass in P9603, just as another four A/S bombs are dropped a mere 100ft from the U-boat.

Left: An unknown seriously damaged U-boat somewhere in the mid-Atlantic, destined never to return to its home base.

Below: U-461, U-462 and U-504 photographed in position 45°40'N 10°55'W from 228 Squadron Mk III JM679.

Bottom: 461 Squadron Sunderland Mk III W6077, flown by Flt Lt D. Marrows DSO, DFC, sunk U-461 on 30 July 1943.

Right: Flt Lt D Marrows DSO, DFC, of 461 Squadron RAAF.

Below left: The commander of U-461 was KrvKpt Wolf Stiebler, who was saved by a dinghy dropped by Flt Lt Marrows.

Below right: Aircrew cling to the remains of Sunderland Mk III W4020 whilst HMS *Wren* comes alongside on 1 August 1943.

U-106 lies motionless in the water, photographed from Fg Off Hanbury's Sunderland Mk III JM708 on 2 August 1943.

Above: As U-106 settles in the water, Sunderland Mk III DV698 flown by Flt Lt I. Clarke DFC prepares a final attack on the crippled U-boat.

Left: The crew of U-426 begin to enter the water, but, unfortunately, no rescue came and all 51 perished.

Below: Photographed by the navigator of Sunderland Mk III EK575, the final moments of U-571 are captured after the attack by Flt Lt R. D. Lucas on 28 January 1944.

Another view of U-571 appearing to explode, 180 miles west of Iceland, taking all 52 crew to the bottom of the Atlantic Ocean.

Right: Flt Lt S. W. Butler DFC in Sunderland Mk III EK591 of 422 Squadron scores a direct hit on U-625 on 10 March 1944.

Below: Despite the vast majority of the 53 crew abandoning U-625, all would lose their lives to the icy waters of the Atlantic.

422 Squadron Mk III EK591 rests between sorties at Castle Archdale in early 1944. The flying boat went on to serve with 4 OTU in July 1944, before heading for 57 Maintenance Unit (MU) at Wig Bay a year later. Declared surplus, this loyal Sunderland was SOC on 2 November 1945. (Via Martyn Chorlton)

Fg Off T. F. P. Frizell was carrying out a tour of duty away from operational flying with 4 OTU when he came across U-675 off the Norwegian coast on 24 May 1944. His attack was clinical, and the demise of the U-boat and its crew was quick.

Above left: Flt Lt L. H. Baveystock scores his first U-boat kill on a moonlit night on 7 June 1944, sinking U-955 100 miles north of Carino, Spain.

Above right: Hans-Heinrich Ketels was one of the 14 survivors from U-970, sunk on 7 June 1944. He went on to command U-2523, U-3511 and U-1162 before the war's end.

Below: U-243 under attack 230 miles west of Nantes by Fg Off W. B. Tilley's Sunderland Mk III W4020 of 10 Squadron RAAF.

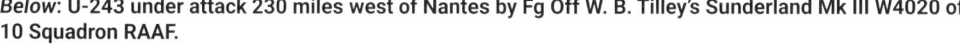

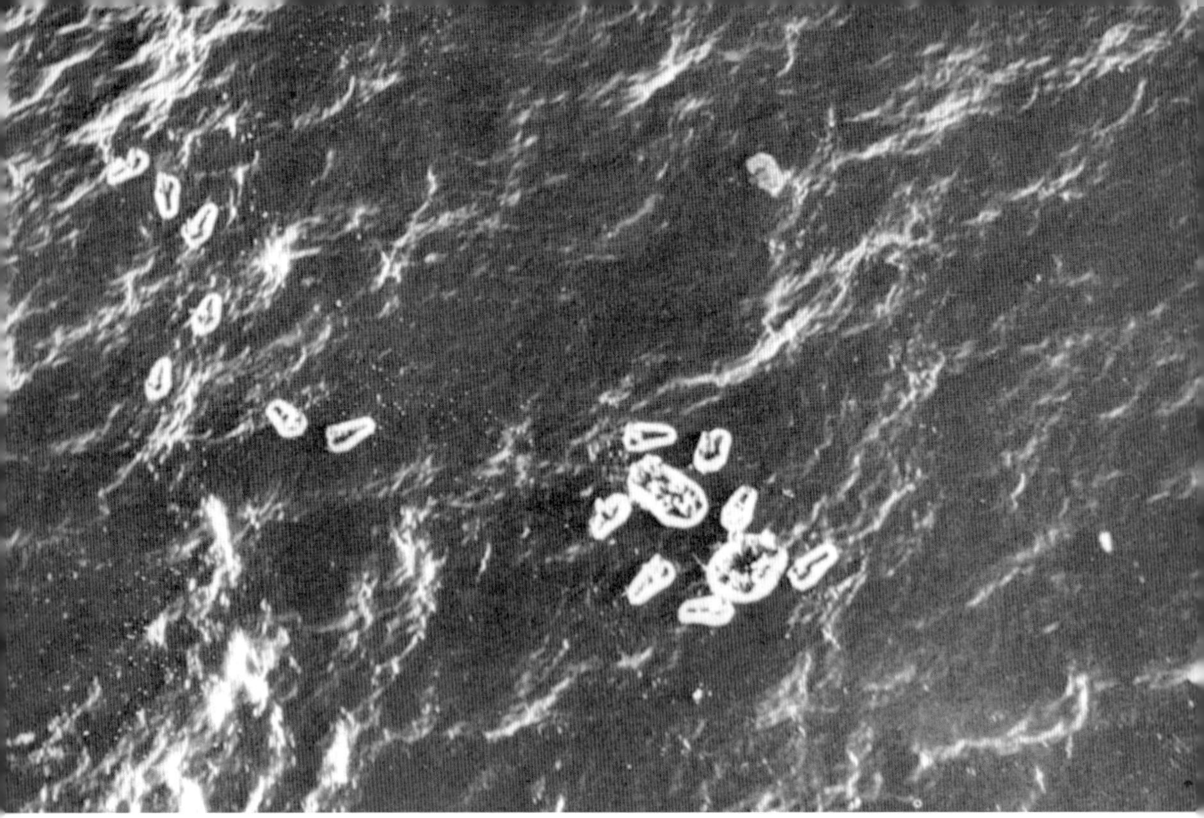

Above: Thirty-eight of the U-boat crew, including the crew of U-243, were rescued by HMCS *Restigouche*.

Below left: Flt Lt W. B. 'Bill' Tilley DFC of 10 Sqn RAAF.

Below right: Flt Lt L. H. Baveystock DSO, DFC Bar, DFM 201 Sqn, who was credited with sinking U-955 and the elusive U-107.

A pair of Spitfires accompany a Coastal Command Sunderland as it heads out into the mid-Atlantic on another long anti-submarine patrol in July 1944. (*Aeroplane*)

U-71 being strafed during Flt Lt S. R. C. Wood's second pass in W3986 on 5 June 1942. The U-boat escaped with damage, later limping into La Pallice.

U-518 during the first of two attacks it suffered in the space of three days. This photo was taken from Sunderland Mk III flown by Fg Off B. H. Layne of 201 Squadron. The U-boat was lucky to escape.

Above left and above right: Skilful evasive manoeuvring by U-119's commander, KptLt Horst-Tessen von Kameke, saved the boat from destruction.

Right: KrvKpt Peter-Erich Cremer was commander of U-333 from 18 May 1943 to 19 July 1944. He handed the reins over to KptLt Hans Fiedler and, within ten days, the U-boat was sunk in the North Atlantic by HMS *Starling* and HMS *Loch Killin*.

Below: Completely obscured by the spray from one of the six depth charges dropped around it on 20 July 1944, U-387 was very lucky to survive Lt B. Thurmann-Nielson's attack.

Sunderland Mk II W3986 saw a great deal of action – all with 10 Sqn RAAF, which it joined on 28 August 1941. The Sunderland was mysteriously lost on 20 May 1943, when it crashed in flames near Eddystone Lighthouse with the loss of all 12 aircrew on board.

SUNDERLANDS SHOT DOWN BY U-BOATS

24 May 1943 – U-441 and/or U-594 shot down Mk III EJ139 of 228 Squadron flown by Fg Off H. J. Debnam over the Bay of Biscay at 2050hrs. EJ139 was hit heavily during its attack run, but still managed to drop five depth charges. All 11 aircrew on board the Sunderland were killed.

13 June 1943 – U-564 and/or U-634 shot down 228 Squadron Sunderland flown Fg Off L. B. Lee. Possibly brought down by the combined flak of five U-boats northwest of Cape Finisterre. Fg Off Lee singled out U-564 and dropped depth charges but crashed in flames only moments later; all 11 aircrew on board were killed.

1 August 1943 – U-454 shot down Mk III W4020 of 10 Squadron RAAF flown by Flt Lt K. G. Fry. It crashed in the Bay of Biscay.

4 August 1943 – U-489 shot down Mk III DD859 of 423 Squadron flown by Fg Off A. A. Bishop.

Three beautiful boats in a row, although the one in the foreground, Sunderland prototype K4774, can fly too! (*Aeroplane*)

17 October 1943 – U-448 shot down Mk III JM712 of 422 Squadron flown by Flt Lt P. T. Sargent. It was ditched roughly 250 miles south of Iceland.

20 November 1943 – U-648 shot down Mk III W6031 of 422 Squadron flown by Fg Off J. D. B. Ulrichson. The aircraft is presumed ditched 150 miles west of Gibraltar.

24 May 1944 – U-921 shot down Mk III DV990 of 422 Squadron flown by Fg Off G. E. Holley. The Sunderland crashed into the sea and all 12 aircrew on board were killed.

11 June 1944 – U-228 shot down a 228 Squadron Sunderland.

11 June 1944 – U-333 shot down 228 Squadron ML880 being flown by Flt Lt M. E. Slaughter.

12 June 1944 – U-333 shot down 201 Squadron Sunderland 'S'.

ITALIAN SUBMARINES SUNK OR DAMAGED BY SUNDERLANDS

Anfrinite – 28 June 1940 – Damaged by Wg Cdr Nicholetts of 228 Squadron 70 miles southwest of Zakynthos (Zante), Greece.

Argonauta – 28 June 1940 – Sunk by Flt Lt Campbell of 230 Squadron off Alexandria in L5804.

Rubino – 29 June 1940 – Sunk by Flt Lt Campbell of 230 Squadron 75 miles southwest of Kerkyra in L5804. Campbell picked up four survivors.

Unknown Italian Submarine – 12 July 1940 – Sqn Ldr G. L. Menzies of 228 Squadron claimed to have sunk an Italian submarine on this day. No record.

Gondar – 30 September 1940 – Shared sinking by Flt Lt P. H. Allington of 230 Squadron in L2166 with HMAS *Stuart* 45 miles off the Egyptian coast.

Marcello – 6 January 1941 – Claimed sunk by Flt Lt Baker of 210 Squadron in P9624, 350 miles west of the Outer Hebrides. *Marcello* was officially sunk on 22 February by HMS *Montgomery*.

Delfino – 1 August 1941 – Damaged by Flt Lt Brand of 230 Squadron off the Libyan coast. The Sunderland was subsequently shot down and some of the crew became POWs.

Argo – 28 May 1942 – Damaged Fg Off H. G. Pockley of 10 Squadron RAAF in W3983 40 miles northwest of Caxine. Combined attack with at least two Hudsons.

Luigi Torello – 7 June 1942 – Damaged by Plt Off T. A. Egerton in W3994 and Flt Lt E. St. C. Yeoman in W4019, both of 10 Squadron RAAF. The submarine was forced to divert to Santander, Spain, for repairs.

Otaria – 13 June 1942 – Damaged by Sqn Ldr R. Burrage of 202 Squadron in W4028/B.

Reginaldo Guiliano – 1 September 1942 – Attacked by Ft Lt S. R. C. Wood in W3986/U and Fg Off H. G. Pockley in W3983/R, both of 10 Squadron RAAF. A Wellington of 304 Squadron also joined the attack, 170 miles off Gironde. The submarine's commander was killed in the attack, which forced the boat to divert to Santander for repairs.

Alabastro – 14 September 1942 – Sunk by Flt Lt E. P. Walshe (RAAF) of 202 Squadron in W6002/R near Algiers. Approximately 40 survivors were spotted in the sea after the attack.

Chapter 6
We Search and Strike

It was with only minimal Nazi pomp and ceremony that U-boat U-489 prepared to leave Kiel on its first patrol on Thursday 22 July 1943. U-489 was one of just ten 1,600-ton Type XIV supply U-boats, nicknamed 'Milk Cows', which were specifically designed to resupply the fighting U-boats. They had no offensive armament, but they were more than capable of defending themselves from the air.

U-489 was under the command of Oblt Adalbert Schmandt, a man whose main experience came from ten years' service with the German Merchant Navy before World War Two. He had ridden on the success of the Nazi party, had been a fully paid-up member since its formation and was not averse to reminding his crew of that fact.

Accompanied by a 500-ton U-boat and a pair of Minesweepers providing an escort, the group arrived at Kristiansand South on 23 July. Taking on just fresh water, the small group continued the following day before stopping at Egersund. The U-boats then continued to the Rosengarten before finally parting company and setting out on their respective patrol areas. For U-489, though, the journey was interrupted when it stopped to pick up the three-man crew of a BV 138 that had been shot down by a 404 (RCAF) Squadron Beaufighter. It was not an easy passage through the Rosengarten, as U-489 had to spend more time under the surface than planned to avoid Allied aircraft and ships intent on restricting U-boat movement. Having traversed the Norwegian Sea, U-489's crew would have been relieved to have made it as far as south of Iceland before the first attack began.

The first aircraft to spot the U-boat was a Catalina IB of 190 Squadron, being flown by Flt Lt B. Crosland in support of an unidentified RAF Flying Fortress. The Fortress did not attack but Crosland carried out a strafing run on the surfaced U-boat and was hit twice by defending flak from U-489. With a damaged radio compartment and near-severed rudder cables, the Catalina jettisoned its depth charges and limped back to Reykjavik. As the Catalina turned away, a Hudson of 269 Squadron, also operating from Reykjavik and flown by Flt Sgt E. L. J. Brame, attacked the U-boat from 3,000ft with a pair of 100lb A/S bombs. While these fell 30 yards port of the enemy boat, it appears that they caused some damage and, after crash-diving to avoid the Hudson, U-489 was not brought back under control until it reached a depth of 656ft. With water entering the forward battery hatch, U-489 had no choice but to surface again.

At Castle Archdale in Northern Ireland, Fg Off Albert A. Bishop, RCAF, and his ten-man crew of 423 Squadron prepared for a shuttle patrol to Reykjavik. Covering a patrol line from the northern-most island of the Hebrides direct to the Icelandic capital, these sorties were more popular than having to trawl all the way back to Northern Ireland in a single sortie. On the afternoon of 3 August, the crew were informed that they would probably be called upon to fly a Moorings patrol the following day, so an earlier than usual night was in order. Their aircraft, Sunderland Mk III DD859, 'G' for George, had been with Bishop and his crew since it was delivered from the factory just over 40 days previously. More than 200 flying hours had already been accumulated and the engineers were keen to carry out an engine change at the same time, as the crew was due for some leave.

Woken at 0300hrs on 4 August, the crew of 11 were delivered to the operations block, fed and watered before getting on with the now familiar task of planning their sortie. During the briefing, they were informed that a U-boat had been attacked in the region they would be patrolling, but they took very little notice as the chances of spotting an enemy vessel in these waters were rare. With the first signs of dawn now beginning to show, the crew walked to Castle Archdales pier, where they were collected by dinghy and delivered to DD859 at rest on Lough Erne. Just before 0500hrs, the lumbering Sunderland lifted from the lake and the navigator, Plt Off H. B. Parliament, gave Bishop a course straight out for St John's Point. Then it was on towards Rothlin O'Birne, before setting a northerly course to pick up the beginning of the patrol. At 0859hrs, the course was altered to a north-westerly direction and, at 4,000ft, the aircraft's autopilot was engaged.

Albert Bishop recorded the events in detail:

> On the afternoon of 3 August 1943, the Flight Commander informed us that there was a trip on our squadron, doing a Moorings patrol, and landing in Iceland, to return on another job at a later date. It was to be our last job before leave, and they were also anxious to get the hours on the aircraft, so they could do an engine change.
>
> We rolled in fairly early that evening and were awakened the next morning at 0300hrs by the batman. After dressing we walked over to the mess where the transport picked us up and took us down to the operations block. There we had a meal and carried out the usual procedure of

A 423 Squadron Sunderland Mk II rests on the edge of Lough Erne while three more are moored on the water. 423 Squadron served at Castle Archdale from 2 November 1942 through to 8 August 1945. (Via Martyn Chorlton)

preparing for a trip. In the operations room they informed us that there had been a U-boat sighted the previous day in the area we were to cover.

From the operations block we walked to the pier where we waited a few minutes for a dinghy to take us to our aircraft. There were a few clouds in the sky, and first signs of dawn were showing to the North-East. Everything went along well, we boarded the aircraft and carried out the necessary checks. Everything was in order.

The engines were then started and we taxied out for take-off, were airborne shortly before 0500hrs, and set course straight out for St John's Point. When we reached the light there we could see Rothlin O'Birne light.

From Rothlin O'Birne we set course North, for a point [from] which we would commence our patrol. We were expecting to come across a convoy and a sea force on our way, so picked them up on our special equipment and passed slightly east of them just before dawn, although we couldn't see them.

Around 0700hrs I sighted something off on the starboard bow, so we immediately dove down towards it, to find that it was a small fishing trawler steaming along in a south-easterly direction.

At 0859hrs we altered course to patrol in a north-westerly direction, and I took over the controls. We were at 4,000ft, 'George' was put to work, all was peaceful, and the air was smooth.

Right: A very appropriate emblem for U-489 was this bear drinking milk. (Via Martyn Chorlton)

Below: Sunderland Mk III 'L' of 423 Squadron at rest at Castle Archdale in 1943.

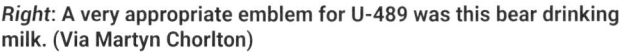

Fg Off Albert A. Bishop's crew on the wing of their aircraft.

Albert Bishop (second from left, pouring) is joined by Peter Frizell (leaning over with glass on right), who sank U-675 whilst 'off ops' with 4 OTU on 24 May 1944. Standing at the rear right and smiling directly at the camera is Harry Parliament, Bishop's navigator.

Fg Off A. E. 'Art' Mountford at his wireless operator's station on board DD859.

U-489

Type: XIV. Builder: F. Krupp Germaniawerft AG, Kiel (werk 558). Ordered: 17 July 1941. Laid Down: 28 January 1942. Launched: 24 December 1942. Commissioned: 8 March 1943.

Commander: Oblt Adalbert Schmandt (I/40) (born 26 December 1909, Wustrow, Rostock. Died 1958). Promoted to Oblt on 1 June 1943. Served with 4 Flottile (training) from 8 March 1943 to 31 July 1943 and 12 Flottile (front boat) from 1–4 August 1943. POW from 4 August 1943 to April 1947.

Patrols: Left Kiel 22 July 1943 and lost bound for refuelling operations.

Description: Designed as an ocean-going tanker to refuel and resupply smaller U-boats, the Type XIV had ten watertight compartments and fuel oil was carried in a large outer hull. The U-boat had a diving depth of 100/240m (300/720ft) and had a length of 67.1m, a height of 11.7m and a draught of 6.51m. The boat had a surfaced displacement of 1,688 tons and 1,932 tons submerged. It could travel at 14kts surfaced or just 6kts submerged and had a range of 12,350 miles at 10kts surfaced or, a mere 55 miles at 4kts submerged.

The U-boat was unarmed, with the exception of a pair of 37mm and a single 20mm anti-aircraft gun for self-defence. Post mid-1943, additional 20mm guns were fitted to the bridge. Four torpedoes could be carried inside a pressurised container behind the bridge for the use of other U-boats, and bunkers could hold up to 432 tons of diesel fuel. Complement of the Type XIV was six officers and 47 ratings.

Action Stations!

The peace was then shattered at 0915hrs when Bishop sounded 'action stations' after he spotted a U-boat on the surface, approximately five miles off the port bow. The crew responded instantly; the depth charges were run out on their rails under the wing and the first wireless operator, Fg Off A. E. 'Art' Mountford instinctively began sending a first sighting report back to base. Unaware of U-489's battery hatch predicament, Bishop presumed that the boat was employing a new kind of defensive tactic by staying surfaced. By now U-489's batteries were exhausted after having to avoid another attack – this time by a Royal Navy destroyer – giving it no choice but to slug it out on the surface with the Sunderland.

As Bishop approached the U-boat, it took evasive action by turning back and forth, always keeping its stern flak gun towards the aircraft. While this manoeuvring continued, Bishop remained about a mile away from the U-boat and, at approximately 600ft above the calm water, tried fruitlessly to force the enemy boat into making an error. Finally, Bishop began his attack out of the sun, three quarters of a mile away from the U-boat and just 300ft above the water. At this point, the Sunderland had room to manoeuvre, and one crewman began opening fire with a single 0.5in Browning on a swivel in the nose at 1,000 yards, registering several early hits on the conning tower. Bishop jinked the giant flying boat from side to side in an effort to avoid the enemy's fire, which at this stage was not quite finding its mark. With 500 yards to run, the second wireless operator, Sgt H. E. Finn opened up the two 0.303 in Brownings in the nose turret and Bishop descended to 50ft for the attack run. At this point in any Sunderland attack, those not gainfully employed had to just sit it out as the U-489's flak gunners began to find their target. The prickly 'Milk Cow' not only sported a 4.7in flak gun but also at least four

20mm cannon and several multi-calibre machine guns. At the 300-yard point, the enemy fire seemed to pour through the flying boat and casualties were now being taken by Bishop's crew. The first was possibly 20-year-old Sgt Frank 'Ginger' Hadcroft, DD859's rigger, who was hit in the head by a single round from a German Luger. At the front of the flying boat, the second pilot, Fg Off Murray Wettlaufer, and the flight engineer, Sgt P. McDonnell, were both injured when shrapnel ripped through the cockpit. Gauges went haywire and the flying controls became difficult but the Browning in the nose kept firing while Sgt Finn's guns lay silent. The whole of the front turret had been taken out by a 4.7in shell but, remarkably, Finn, although seriously injured, had survived. There then followed a second shudder as another 4.7in shell slammed into the port wing between the two Pegasus engines.

Despite the chaos going on all around him, Bishop remained focused on his quarry and, at 140kts and 50ft above U-489, he released six Mk IX Torpex depth charges directly along the track of the enemy. At this point it was clear to Bishop that DD889 was not going to fly much further. The enemy fire, especially within the last 100 yards of the attack run, had done more than enough to ensure that this crew would not be flying on to Iceland. There was fire raging in the bomb-room and galley and the port wing was well ablaze. The ailerons were unresponsive, and the trimming tabs had been shot away, making controlled flight near impossible. Bishop was also conscious of the threat of explosion as the fires spread, making ditching in short order the only option. Bishop describes what happened next:

> … We bounced once, twice, three times on the swell, and after the third bounce the port wing dropped… The float was torn off, the wing-tip dug in, and the kite cart wheeled into the sea. One second there was a crash and the next we found ourselves in the water… The port wing had disappeared and a fire blazed where it should have been. The starboard wing (now also on fire) and the fuselage were still afloat. One of the boys sat on the tailplane for a while but soon had to swim for it as the Sunderland went down within five minutes of hitting.

On impact, Murray Wettlaufer was launched out of the aircraft through the cockpit window and found himself swimming in a sea covered in burning aviation fuel. Bishop surfaced to see his Sunderland lying broken on the surface with at least one of the crew sitting on the tailplane; after less than five minutes the entire aircraft had slipped beneath the waves. Bishop swam over to the seriously injured Sgt Finn (a non-swimmer who was not wearing a life jacket) and tried to use one of the aircraft's floats to support him. However, it soon sank and, although injured in the arm and in great pain, Bishop kept Finn afloat until rescue came. All the crew who could be accounted for were from the front end of the aircraft, including all three wireless operators, the two pilots and the flight engineer.

With no dinghy to climb into, the survivors huddled together in the open ocean and watched as events a few hundred yards away began to unfold. U-489 had been steadily approaching for quite some time, with its stern down and what seemed to be virtually all the crew standing out on the foredeck. They had been making a vain attempt to right the crippled vessel, but once the U-boat was within 200 yards of the Sunderland crew, the German sailors took to their large and comfortable inflatable lifeboats. Behind them, the stern of U-489 continued to settle in the water until the bow began to rise to angle of 30°. Once this point was reached, the U-boat finally gave up and was ripped apart by a huge explosion leaving virtually nothing behind. Two more underwater explosions followed along with the German crew's defiant shouts of 'Seig heil! Seig heil!' before the calm of the sea returned. Now just a mere 100 yards apart, the crews of the U-boat and the Sunderland eyed each other with caution. Little concern was shown towards the RCAF and RAF airmen shivering in the open water, despite the fact that there was room to take them on board. However, the airmen did have the advantage of knowing that the chances of being rescued by an Allied vessel were considerably higher than being lifted from the sea by a German ship.

Right: Murray Wettlaufer at the controls of 'his own' Sunderland flying boat.

Below: The hopelessly exposed crew of a U-Boat in the North Atlantic attempt to take cover during an aerial attack in 1943.

Rescue

Unbeknown to the Sunderland crew, Royal Navy destroyers HMS *Castleton* and *Orwell* had seen the flying boat attack and its subsequent crash-landing into the sea. *Castleton* made good speed to the men in the sea and rescued the six very cold and tired airmen from the water, as well as 58 Germans from the U-489. Only one German officer, Sub Lt Nude, was seriously injured following the first explosion on the U-boat and succumbed not long after his rescue on HMS *Orwell*.

HMS *Castleton* steered at full speed for Iceland and the nearest hospital, but time was of the essence and the ship's doctor had no choice but to operate on Murray Wettlaufer and Sgt Finn, no doubt saving their lives in the process. Bishop had the unpleasant job of identifying 'Ginger' Hadcroft's body – the only one recovered from the sea. Sgt Hadcroft was then committed back into the sea to join WO John Stanley Kelly, Plt Off Harry Bertram Parliament, Flt Sgt J. B. Horsburgh and Sgt Herbert Gossop.

These five casualties were the first suffered in 352 operational sorties by 423 Squadron since its formation in May 1942. The destruction of U-489 was the second for the squadron, which would go on to sink a total of five, making 423 Squadron the most successful RCAF unit in this field of operations. The squadron can proudly display on its banner not only the Atlantic 1942–45 battle honour but also Biscay 1944, Normandy 1944 and English Channel and North Sea 1944–45, showing clearly how vast an area of operations this outstanding squadron covered.

HMS *Castleton* (Left) and HMS *Orwell* (Below), the two Royal Navy destroyers that came to the rescue of the surviving crew of the Sunderland and 58 German U-Boat crew.

DESCRIPTIONS FROM THE INTERROGATION REPORT OF U-489'S OFFICERS CARRIED OUT IN SEPTEMBER 1943

'U-489 carried a complement of 54 officers and men, including two engineer officers and a Surgeon-Lieutenant. They were one of the poorest U-boat crews yet encountered. All the officers except one were lower deck promotions ('Volksoffizier') for some of whom other officer prisoners felt constrained to apologise, and the average experience and intelligence among the men was appallingly low... A high degree of stupid, mulish security-consciousness prevailed, combined with an almost total lack of manners in both officers and men.'

Captain: 'He was a man of little education. He was a long standing member of the Nazi party, having joined during a three year period of unemployment before Hitler's rise to power, and was full of gratitude for what the party had done for him. He had set and lofty ideas on the duties of an officer and managed to inoculate a high degree of security consciousness in his crew.'

First Lieutenant – Gerhard Schultz: 'He was a dull, sullen and uninteresting type. His security consciousness was difficult to distinguish from mental incompetence, and his manners were boorish.'

Second Lieutenant - Hans Vitt: '... a most unprepossessing and unkempt ex-Merchant Navy seaman and naval rating. He spoke very passable English and tried to compensate for his complete lack of background and poise by aping the Prussian officer type.'

Junior Engineering Officer – Friedrich Bickenbach: 'He was an overbearing, pink-faced Hitler Youth product who had to be taught the elements of civil behaviour before it was possible to talk to him at all! He knew little and said even less.'

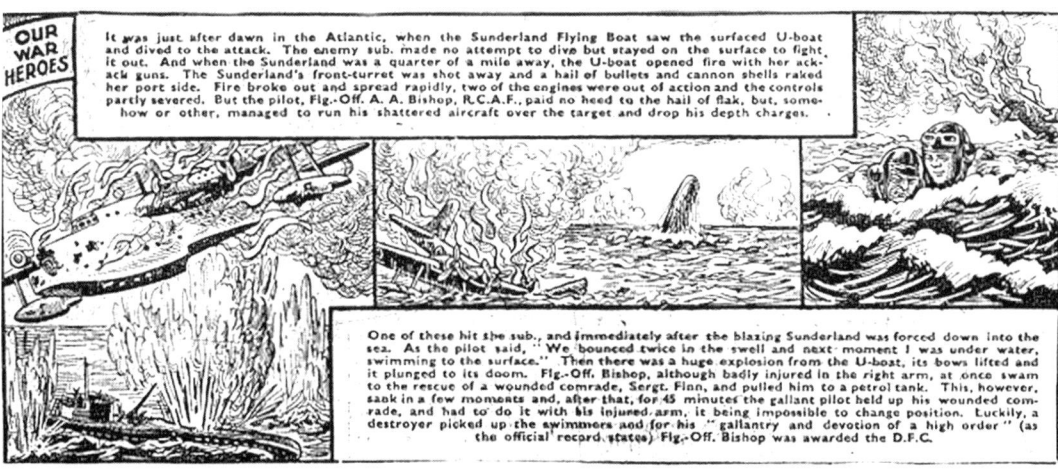

Above: The battle with U-489 on 31 August 1943 was well publicised at the time, including this 'comic-strip' description of the day's events.

Right: The first production Sunderland Mk I, L2158, on the River Medway in April 1938. After trials with the MAEE and a brief spell with BOAC, the Sunderland entered service with 204 Squadron. Coded 'KG-M', the flying boat was lost on 17 August 1942 whilst on convoy escort from Bathurst. (*Aeroplane* via Martyn Chorlton)

Chapter 7

The 'Flying Boat Union' Lives On

Cessation and demobilisation

With the end of the war in Europe in May 1945, Coastal Command took a step back to reorganise its squadrons and assess its own operational future. The role of peacetime general reconnaissance would see a rapid run down of the Sunderland squadrons within the command and from April to October 1945: 10, 95, 204, 228, 259, 270, 422, 423, 461 and 490 squadrons had been disbanded and 330 and 343 squadrons transferred to the Norwegian and French air forces, respectively. By 1 January 1946, only 201, 205, 209, 230 and 240 squadrons were still operational Sunderland units, although the latter had also fallen by the wayside at Koggala on 13 March 1946. 88 Squadron would bolster the Sunderland strength from 1 September 1946, when it was reformed from 1430 Flight at Kai Tak.

Despite the peace that now descended upon the world, there was still the need for the RAF to maintain communications throughout the British Empire and fly the flag where needed. The Sunderlands were, by now, the only flying boats in RAF service and, with a projected service life extending into the 1950s, the need to maintain a training unit for future aircrew was still required. The main wartime training unit was 4 (C)OTU (Coastal), which was formed back in 1941. The OTU was transferred from Alness to Pembroke Dock on 15 August 1946, followed by another move to Calshot in July 1947 where the unit was renamed as 235 OCU (Operational Conversion Unit) under the command of Sqn Ldr D. B. Fitzpatrick. 201 and 230 squadrons had already established themselves at Calshot the previous year, which left 88 Squadron at Kai Tak, 205 Squadron at Koggala and 209 Squadron at Seletar.

A 230 Squadron Sunderland Mk V photographed en route to the RAF Pageant. (Charles E Brown)

Sunderland Mk V SZ568 of 235 OCU on a training sortie off the Cornish coast.

The Far East and the 'Yangtse Incident'

For the Far East-based Sunderland squadrons, the first and primary tasking was to help evacuate Allied POWs who had suffered in the Japanese camps. The role later developed into a general freight and passenger-carrying service throughout the Far East. Loads would vary from the mundane, such as mail, medical supplies and food, although the last did involve one Sunderland carrying a full load just of curry for some Indian soldiers. On another occasion, a Sunderland was used to transport several Japanese war criminals who were guarded by a detail of Ghurkas with their kukris unsheathed!

88 Squadron was by far the busiest of the three Far Eastern squadrons. Under the command of Wg Cdr W. E. Ogle-Skan AFC, all of the squadron's Sunderlands were converted to carry 20 passengers and stripped of all gun turrets. 88 Squadron continued its transport and freight role until April 1948, having carried 2,368 passengers and over 200,000lb of stores. The squadron's Sunderlands were then reconverted back to a more militarised role and returned to general reconnaissance duties, now under the command of Sqn Ldr D. M. Gall DFC.

Gall was delivering a Sunderland back to the UK for major maintenance when one of his aircraft became involved in an international 'incident'. On 21 April 1949, HQ FEAF (Far East Air Force) received a signal from HMS *Amethyst* stating that it had been fired upon, had suffered casualties and damage and was forced to run aground on the banks of the Yangtse River. With a hole in its hull, the ship had come under fire from People's Liberation Army (PLA) forces, causing severe damage. *Amethyst* was in big trouble, especially when HMS *Blake* and *London* tried to reach it and failed. It was now the turn of 88 Squadron and, flying Sunderland Mk V ML772, Flt Lt K. Letford DSO, DFC spent the next five days landing alongside the crippled ship, even though Chinese gunfire continued, hitting the aircraft several times. Letford delivered an RAF medical officer, a Royal Navy chaplain and a replacement crew for the ship and supplies. Sunderland Mk V NJ176 was also involved in the final airborne relief supply to the ship, which managed to run the gauntlet of the Chinese batteries and eventually return safely to the UK. Letford was awarded a Bar to his DFC and all the Sunderland aircrew involved received the Naval General Service Medal.

Above: RN303, a Mk V serving with 209 Squadron, at Seletar in 1948. RN303 was one of the few Sunderlands that nearly saw the age of the RAF flying boat come to an end, being SOC on 24 January 1959. (Via Martyn Chorlton)

Left: PP127 'L' whilst serving with 205 Squadron, which became 205/209 Squadron/detachment in 1955. Mk V PP127 joined 205/209 Squadron on 1 April 1957 and was SOC on 1 June 1959. (Via Martyn Chorlton)

Only a fortnight after the 'Yangtse Incident', 88 Squadron was again called upon to carry out a mercy mission as Chinese troops closed on Shanghai on 14 May 1949. This time, Sqn Ldr Gall flew a Sunderland to Shanghai to evacuate 26 British nationals to Hong Kong. Flt Lt Letford evacuated 38 servicemen on 16 May and, two days later, collected 35 more. The following day, a final Sunderland trip rescued 22 refugees from the city, which was overrun by communists a few days later.

Operation *Plainfare*

Back in the UK, 201, 230 and 235 OCU were all preparing themselves for a much bigger mercy mission under the name Operation *Plainfare* (first codenamed Carter Paterson), better known as the Berlin Airlift. Ever since January 1948, the Soviets had been closing down all surface access into West Berlin, effectively stifling the British, French and American-controlled sectors of the city. The blockade was complete by 24 June and the only way to get in and out of the city was by flying down a few narrow airways from West Germany. Over two million people (civilians and thousands of Allied occupation forces) needed to be fed and supplied and, in anticipation, the RAF and USAF began a huge, well organised freight airlift into West Berlin.

The RAF made its first flight on 30 June and, until the Soviets lifted the blockade on 12 May 1949, the vast majority of supplies into the city were brought in by civil and military landplanes, along with the valuable contribution made by the RAF's Sunderlands. During the airlift, the three squadrons operated under a single temporary wing at Finkenwerder on the River Elbe, Hamburg, under the command of Wg Cdr J. L. Crosbie. The flying boats' destination was the Havel, a linear expansion of the river that passed through West Berlin but also traversed the British and Soviet sectors. There was no margin for error with regard to navigation and, on landing, the Sunderlands' cargo was immediately unloaded into barges and taken ashore for distribution. The Havel, surrounded by low hills, was a challenging place to land a large flying boat; the water was always calm, and the landing area was very long, but only on one heading. This meant that the majority of take-off and landings were made with a crosswind.

The Sunderland was a very useful aircraft for large freight and, during the airlift, was used a great deal for bulk loads of salt which, when carried by landplanes, caused untold mayhem to any component that would corrode. A typical load (up to 10,000lb of salt) would be stowed in the lower deck area and bomb compartments.

The first Sunderland operations into Berlin began on 5 July 1948, and it was not long before an average of 16 sorties a day was achieved. The sight of giant flying boats was very novel to the Berlin population and equally bemusing to the Soviets looking on. People would line the banks of the Havel by the hundreds, if not thousands, to watch the aircraft come and go and one was quoted as saying, 'Your Sunderlands have aroused utter amazement among the Ivans'.

The average turnaround time after landing for a typical Sunderland delivery was 20 minutes but the record off-loading time was made on 9 December when 12 men relieved the flying boat of 10,020lb of salt in just 3mins and 12secs!

By December 1948, the Havel had frozen over, and the three Sunderland squadrons returned to Calshot on 14 December. During this period, the three units had flown more than 1,000 sorties and 4,487 tons of freight had been flown into Berlin. The Sunderlands also brought 1,113 starving German children back to the UK. Salt, unsurprisingly, was the biggest amount of foodstuff flown into Berlin at 2,500 tons.

There was a plan for the Sunderlands to return to Berlin in spring 1949 once the ice on the Havel had melted. By then, though, the circuit around the nearby airfield at Gatow was choked with aircraft and the increased use of Berlin Tegel Airport did not warrant the use of the water-based Sunderland anymore. 201 Squadron was then moved to Pembroke Dock in January 1949, followed by 230 Squadron in February, while 235 OCU resumed its training role from Calshot.

230 Squadron Sunderland Mk V RN299 moored on the River Thames, off the Greenwich Naval College in June 1946. (*Aeroplane*)

Above: Mk V SZ577 whilst serving with 88 Squadron in the Far East. By 1950, the flying boat was at Wig Bay with 57 MU, followed by 201 Squadron, 209 Squadron and finally 205/209 Squadron before being SOC on 24 May 1957.

Left: 201 Squadron Mk V 'D' being unloaded on Lake Havel, during Operation *Plainfare* in August 1948.

An unknown Sunderland taking part in the Berlin Airlift.

Calshot in 1948. On view
are Sunderlands of 201 and
230 squadrons and 235 OCU.
Only the last remained there from
1949, while the two squadrons
moved to their final resting place at
Pembroke Dock. (*Aeroplane*)

Right: A fully militarised
209 Squadron Sunderland Mk V
operating over the Far East.

Below: 205/209 Squadron
Sunderland Mk V PP137 over
Singapore in 1956. Within 12
months the aircraft was SOC, and,
not long after, the RAF flying boat
fleet was no more.

Malaya and Operation *Firedog*

While the Berlin Airlift was getting underway in Europe, the situation in the Far East was steadily deteriorating as several civil uprisings began to take hold against their European governors. The most significant of these, for the British at least, was in Malaya where, from 17 June 1948, a state of emergency was declared, and Operation *Firedog* began. The main cause of the problem was the Malayan Communist Party's Army (MCPA) led by Chin Peng, who had actually fought alongside the British against the Japanese during World War Two. Peng's 6,000 strong 'army' was a remnant of the wartime Force 136, which had only part disbanded at the end of the war and still retained a large stock of weapons.

There were no bomber squadrons in the ACSEA (Air Command South East Asia, renamed FEAF in 1949) at the time and the only aircraft capable of dropping ordnance in any great quantity in the theatre was the Sunderland. 209 Squadron at Seletar, under the command of Sqn Ldr P. R. Hatfield DFC, was the only one of the three units capable of operating immediately in a 'heavy' bomber role. The Sunderland crews soon found themselves flying regular bombing sorties against MCPA targets, initially attacked with small fragmentation bombs that were thrown out of the side hatches by hand! This method was soon replaced by proper bomb racks, which not only improved accuracy but also enabled heavier weapons to be carried. 205 Squadron moved to Seletar from Koggala in September 1949 and the two Sunderland units remained the FEAF's heavy bombing force until succeeded by a detachment of 210 Squadron Lancaster ASR.3s flying from St Eval. The following March, the Sunderland 'bombers' were relieved from their improvised tasking when the Lincoln B.2s of 57 Squadron arrived from Waddington, giving the FEAF the bombing clout it needed 18 months earlier. The two Sunderland squadrons still remained in the Malayan theatre but reverted to their original role of maritime and general reconnaissance around the coast, keeping a lookout for suspect vessels transporting equipment to the MCPA.

From 1950, all three Sunderland squadrons were gaining increasing commitments as the Korean War began to gain momentum. All were detached to Iwakuni but Operation *Firedog* sorties were still carried out amidst the Korean duties. 88 Squadron alone had flown 165 *Firedog* sorties before fully committing to the Korean War.

At least 17 Avro Lincolns fly above six Sunderlands during the final stages of Operation *Firedog*. (Aeroplane)

Farewell 'Great White Ships'

While Sunderlands were seeing action in Malaya and operating over Korea, in contrast 201 and 230 squadrons at Pembroke Dock were being called upon for a completely different task. From 1951 to 1954, Sunderlands supported the British Greenland Expedition, which saw the flying boats journey to within 700 miles of the North Pole in very challenging conditions.

Throughout the 1950s, the Sunderlands were regularly called out at a moment's notice to carry out rescue and 'mercy' type operations, often when a landplane would have been of no use. It was while a detachment of 230 Squadron was operating from Malta that a large earthquake hit the Greek Ionian Islands in August 1953. A continuous aid service was immediately set up, with Sunderlands flying medical supplies, emergency personnel, clothing and various supplies to the earthquake zone from 4 August to 2 September.

Responding to call-outs from ships in trouble was another regular task for the Sunderland, but the emergency that occurred 300 miles northeast of Singapore on 19 November 1956 was more challenging than most. Japanese fishing vessel *Feizu Maru* had run into some rocks off the Natuna Islands and was sinking fast. Flt Lt E. C. Donoghue AFC and crew immediately flew across the open sea from Seletar to locate the crippled fishing boat. They then dropped five survival packs, including a large dinghy. Flt Lt Donoghue remained over the scene until the entire 20-man crew was on board the rescue dinghy and a rescue ship was approaching.

By the mid-1950s, each squadron was shrinking as operational requirements and general wear and tear was taking its toll on the ageing flying boats. The Air Ministry policy makers were already planning a completely land-based future for Coastal Command, which would revolve around the Avro Shackleton. It was the UK-based 201 and 230 squadrons that were disbanded first at Pembroke Dock, on 28 February and 31 July 1957, respectively. Their aircraft were flown to 57 Maintenance Unit (MU) at Wig Bay for storage, although a handful were refurbished and despatched to the Far East, while the remainder faced the axe.

Over in Singapore, now affectionately known as the 'Kipper Fleet', the number of Sunderlands had been shrinking since 1954, when 88 Squadron was disbanded at Seletar on 1 October. On 1 January 1955, the

One of the last big displays of RAF Sunderland strength was during the Coronation Flypast over Singapore in 1953.

remains of 205 and 209 squadrons were combined to become 205/209 Squadron under the command of Sqn Ldr D. J. G. Norton. This, in turn, was diluted down again to become 209 Squadron Detachment from 1 March 1958, now under the command of Wg Cdr R. A. N. McCready OBE. With little more than a handful of cherished Sunderlands now airworthy, the hammer finally fell on 15 May 1959 when Mk V DP198 and ML797 made the final flypast over Seletar, marking the end of the 'Kipper Fleet' and the RAF's last flying boats. It was not quite the end though, as the final RAF Sunderland flight was carried out on 20 May, when ML797 flew as an escort to Air Marshal the Earl of Brandon, AOC-in-C, FEAF.

Left: The penultimate Sunderland unit to be disbanded was 201 Squadron at Pembroke Dock on 28 February 1957. (*Flight* via *Aeroplane*)

Below: Lovely aerial view of Calshot in 1948, possibly photographed from a resident Sunderland. The Sunderlands visible are two from 201 Squadron (NS), two from 230 Squadron (4X) and one from 235 OCU (TA), the last remaining here until its disbandment in October 1953. (*Aeroplane*)

Chapter 8

Sunderlands in Korea

The 'Kipper Fleet'

Short Sunderlands were invaluable as long-distance maritime patrol aircraft and accounted for several enemy submarines during World War Two. With the coming of peace, they were assured of a place in the RAF and settled down to routine work, but things changed in 1950.

Communist North Korea decided that all of Korea should follow the Party line and crossed the 38th Parallel into South Korea. This was not a move that the West – particularly the United States – would sanction and a 'conflict' of interests demanded action. The US was heavily involved, but so too were Commonwealth forces including the United Kingdom. Actions by the British Army and the Royal Navy are well documented, but the RAF's role is not so well known. Pilots and aircraft were involved nonetheless, and none more so than those crewing the venerable Sunderland.

There were three squadrons of Sunderlands (88, 205 and 209) that served throughout the Korean campaign. These three units formed the Far East Flying Boat Wing (FEFBW) primarily based at Seletar, Singapore, with detachments rotating between Kai Tak, Hong Kong and Iwakuni, Japan. From 17 June 1948, when Operation *Firedog* commenced, they carried out anti-terrorist patrols over the Malayan jungles and forests over 3,000 miles (4,830km) from base. Rather unkindly, RAF personnel based in the area referred to the FEFBW as the 'Kipper Fleet'.

Following the cessation of hostilities in 1945, the RAF was relegated to a peacetime role, with one of its duties being carrying passengers. In September 1946, 88 Squadron was formed with Sunderlands to meet the weekly BOAC flying boat service from the UK that landed at Kai Tak. From here, the Sunderlands, which had been stripped of their military equipment and fitted with basic seating, took the passengers to Iwakuni, near Hiroshima, Japan. A former Imperial Japanese Naval Air Training School base was used as a terminal for British occupation forces in Japan. Until April 1948, when the service ceased, Sunderlands carried mail and freight, as well as personnel, on the weekly service without missing a flight and with no mishaps of any kind. The aircraft were

Moored at Iwakuni, Japan, is Short Sunderland MR.5 SZ578/B from 88 Squadron during the Korean War. This aircraft was scrapped in October 1957. (John Land and François Prins)

Above: A 209 Squadron Sunderland on the step at Seletar. The unit flew general reconnaissance operations throughout the Korean War. (Via Martyn Chorlton)

Left: A Sunderland Mk V of 230 Squadron on patrol over dense jungle during the early 1950s. (Via Martyn Chorlton)

then returned to normal military fit and resumed their usual Far Eastern duties of patrolling the sea-lanes, performing search and rescue duties and taking part in various exercises in the area, as well as continuing Operation *Firedog* missions.

Crossing the 38th Parallel

It was on one of the exercises in June 1950 that news came of the North Koreans crossing the 38th Parallel into South Korea. The US moved its forces quickly from Japan to South Korea and Britain gave its support, which included the Sunderland squadrons. The flying boats were in action immediately, air-lifting supplies and personnel for the Royal Navy to set up a base at Kure in Japan. The old base at Iwakuni was quickly re-equipped to take the Sunderlands, which would share the marine facilities with USN Martin Mariner flying boats. The first Sunderland to arrive at Iwakuni in June 1950 was 88 Squadron's RN277.

Iwakuni was also a land airfield and was shared by the USAF and the RAAF – the latter already in residence at the time of the outbreak of hostilities. At Iwakuni, the Sunderlands would remain afloat moored to buoys in the artificial harbour created between two breakwaters. Minor services to the aircraft could be carried out in this manner but major work, such as engine or propeller changes, meant fitting the flying boat with beaching gear and having it winched ashore up the slipway. As the hangars at Iwakuni were too small to take the large Sunderland, work had to be carried out in the open. Sunderlands on detachment to Iwakuni brought groundcrew, fitters and engineers with them but local Japanese technicians were also employed as required. Almost all the marine craft, launches and refuelling tenders were manned by Japanese staff, who never failed to work at maximum speed. The Australians and the USAF also used Japanese engineers and fitters on their land-based aircraft, which were based at Iwakuni and could be accommodated in the hangars.

While the RAF was based at Iwakuni, the Sunderlands were under USN tasking, their duties being similar to those of the Mariners. The primary role was maritime reconnaissance – tracking the movements of surface shipping – and reporting their findings back to base. Sunderlands also carried out anti-submarine patrols, a role they performed well even though they sighted no submarines during the entire Korean War. There were three usual patrol areas: the Tsushima Straits (between Japan and Korea), the West Coast (Yellow Sea) and the East Coast (Sea of Japan).

The main task for the flying boats was spotting any shipping in the Tsushima Straits, as this was out of bounds for any enemy vessels. All craft in that area were photographed from the Sunderlands and Mariners and details were passed to the US. Interestingly, the US and RAF crews held a monthly competition for the best photograph taken of shipping, and it was the RAF crews who won more often than their US counterparts. While the flying boats did not get near any of the communist enemy forces, they did occasionally get fired on by US ships and aircraft which obviously could not distinguish the 'Stars-and-bars' on the USN Mariners and the RAF roundels. Fortunately, no serious damage was sustained in the few such incidents recorded.

Right: A 209 Squadron Sunderland Mk V moored at Iwakuni, a particularly useful forward operating base for both RAF and US Navy (USN) flying boats. (Via Martyn Chorlton)

Below: Seen anchored in Iwakuni in 1951 is Sunderland MR.5 SZ599 of 88 Squadron. This aircraft was transferred to 209 Squadron in 1953 and scrapped the following year. (John Land and François Prins)

RAF tender 2961 ferrying the crew of Sunderland SZ578 to their aircraft. (John Land and François Prins)

Left: The port gunner of a Sunderland manning his 0.5in beam gun during a patrol in 1952. Beam guns were fitted when the factory upgraded the Mk III aircraft to MR.5s. (John Land and François Prins)

Below: Three Sunderland MR.5s from 88 Squadron are pictured on patrol during the Korean War. (John Land and François Prins)

The Sunderland in Action

There were only a few occasions during the Korean War when RAF Sunderlands were involved in major actions. One notable event was in September 1950 when General Douglas MacArthur used his Pacific campaign experiences in Korea. Operation *Chromite* was to land an amphibious force of US Marines at Inchon, behind the battlefront to cut off North Korea's supply line and open a second front. Sunderlands from 88 and 209 squadrons were joined by USN P-2 Neptunes of VP-6 to form Task Force 99 Patrol and Reconnaissance Force. Their role was to provide an air umbrella for the assault convoys guarding them against attack from the sea. During the operation, the flying boats maintained day and night patrols without let-up.

Sunderlands from Iwukuni carried out weather patrols at night and also provided anti-submarine protection for Royal Navy craft operating off the Korean coast, which were especially vulnerable when being refuelled or replenished at sea. Happily, there was no submarine action, but the sight of the large flying boat on station was a reassuring presence.

Sunderlands from all three squadrons were tasked with search and rescue missions during the war and, in December 1950, Flt Lt Hunter of 88 Squadron made two open sea landings to rescue 23 crewmen from the Philippine vessel *Joseph S*, which had struck a mine. The rescue was hazardous but successful, and the sailors were flown to Kai Tak where the aircraft landed in almost total darkness. On 15 January 1951, Sunderland RN282 – also from 88 Squadron – under the command of Flt Lt Houtheusen took off to search for USN pilot, Ensign E. J. Hosstra, whose Corsair had been badly damaged in action, causing him to ditch in the sea off Wonsan. When Hosstra was located, he was in his dinghy and quite close to the enemy coast. Flt Lt Houtheusen successfully landed near the dinghy and the exhausted airman was rescued and treated for exposure during the flight back to Iwakuni. When the Sunderland landed back at base, it had been airborne for over 11 hours.

The next day, Sunderland PP155 with Fg Off Brand as captain, was on a routine patrol when they spotted a sampan (a flat-bottomed wooden boat) some 30 miles (50km) off the coast of South Korea. Brand took the flying boat down for a closer look and saw that there were 30 Koreans on board the vessel, which was displaying an SOS signal. Brand then signalled USS *Norris*, which was patrolling nearby, to investigate.

US Navy ships were active in the waters around South Korea and also acted as refuelling points for the Allied flying boats. One of the vessels that carried out this task was USS *Suisan*. This tender was moored off the coast of Korea and the flying boats would land astern and then be pulled near the stern

Sunderland SZ578 on its beaching gear being refuelled at Iwakuni prior to launch for another patrol. The RAF employed Japanese nationals for many ground tasks, including engineers and drivers. (John Land and François Prins)

of the *Suisan* so that refuelling hoses could be connected to the Sunderland or Mariner. The aircraft would be moored for the night and the crews were able to rest aboard the ship or the aircraft as they wished. The next day, the flying boat would carry out another patrol and then return to Iwakuni.

Patrols continued in all weathers and, sadly, some aircraft were lost in accidents. PP154 landed in adverse weather conditions in late 1950 and suffered damage to its wings, floats and tailplane; fortunately, no one was hurt. This cannot be said for Sunderland PP148, which crashed while landing in a heavy sea on 25 March 1953; five crew members were killed. At the end of the year, RN302 from 88 Squadron was lost on 27 December whilst on an anti-submarine patrol in the Tsushima Straits when one engine caught fire and power was lost on another. The aircraft crashed off Tsushima Island.

Above: After a heavy landing in adverse weather conditions, this 209 Squadron Sunderland (PP154) was beached at Oppama in Japan. Re-floated, the aircraft was repaired and continued in service until it was scrapped in 1957. (David Oliver)

Left: Starboard gunner at his beam station with a 0.5in calibre machine gun at the ready. The larger calibre gun replaced the deleted dorsal turret. (John Land and François Prins)

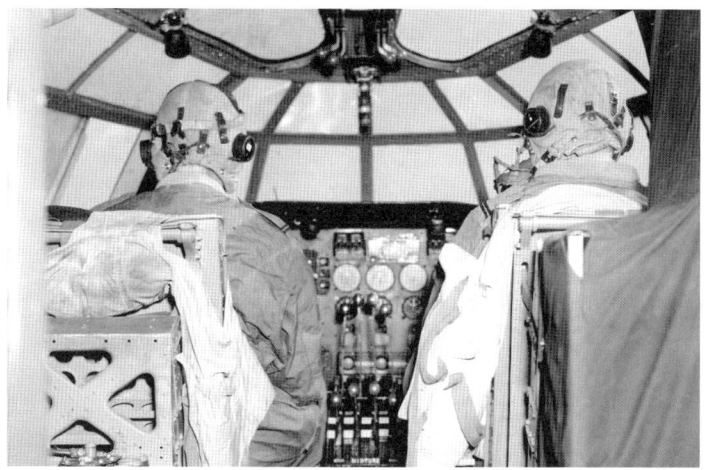

Above left: A British Official Photograph (Air Ministry) extensively captioned as follows: 'C' for Charlie of No. 88 Squadron has been sent by its United States Navy control ship to carry out daylight reconnaissance of Korea's Yellow Sea Coast.

'While the Sunderland flies low over grey seas, its crew scans the horizon for blockade runners. Pilots and gunners keep an uninterrupted lookout while the aircraft's radar scans a much wider sweep of sea. Captain of 'C' for Charlie is Fg Off R S Brand of 8 Calthorpe Mansions, Egbaston, Birmingham, his co-pilot in starboard seat, Fg Off G S Boston of 3 Albany Rd., Leyton, London. E10.' (Crown Copyright via *Aeroplane*)

Above right: Another British Official Photograph (Air Ministry) taken from 'C' for Charlie of 88 Squadron over Korea's Yellow Sea. The caption is: 'One of the Sunderland's mid-upper guns looks out menacingly over the waste of water populated by a lone ship steaming northwards. An obviously friendly vessel, the Sunderland would radio Naval Operations to investigate if suspicions were aroused.' (Crown Copyright via *Aeroplane*)

Ceasefire

A ceasefire in the Korean War was agreed in February 1954 but the flying boats continued their patrols until September of that year. At any time, there were five Sunderlands on detachment at Iwakuni, with duty rotating between the three Seletar-based squadrons. On 2 October 1954, 88 Squadron was disbanded and its aircraft were transferred to 205 and 209 squadrons at Seletar. During the Korean War, the Sunderlands flew patrols on almost every day of the conflict and were the main contribution by the RAF, during that unhappy time.

By 1954, the Sunderland was coming to the end of its RAF service, but it was another five years before the type was officially retired from active duty. A final farewell ceremonial flight over Singapore was flown by two aircraft from 205 Squadron on 14 May 1959. By the end of June, the last Sunderland was struck off charge (SOC) and ended up in the scrapheap at Seletar with several other former 'Kipper Fleet' veterans, many of which had flown missions during the Korean War.

SZ577 of 230 Squadron being prepared for flight at Calshot in 1949. The Sunderland Mk V joined 230 Squadron on 12 September 1947, before being transferred to 88 Squadron in May 1949. A brief spell with 57 MU followed in December 1950, followed by a short tour with 201 Squadron. On 14 July 1954, the flying boat was posted to 209 Squadron, which became 205/209 Squadron in January 1955. This Sunderland was SOC on 24 May 1957. (*Aeroplane*)

Chapter 9

The British North Greenland Expedition

Discovering Greenland

It was 1950 when Cdr C. J. W. Simpson DSC, Royal Navy, visited Greenland for the first time as a guest of Eigil Knuth's Danish Peary Land Expedition. It was during this expedition that Simpson caught sight of a large range of mountains set firmly in inland ice. Located in the northeast of Greenland, Simpson became determined to explore the area, returning the following year with Lt A. B. Erskine, of the Royal Navy.

While Erskine travelled to Greenland by ship, Simpson called upon the services of the RAF to fly his preliminary survey team to the area. Both 201 and 230 squadrons were asked if they could supply a single Sunderland for the operation. 230 Squadron obliged and, on 23 July 1951, Wg Cdr Barrett and Sqn Ldr J. Higgins DFC, AFC (OC 230 Squadron) departed Pembroke Dock with Simpson's party and supplies on board. Eventually, after routing via Reykjavik, the Sunderland became the first RAF aircraft to land in any Greenland fjord – alighting in one off Ella Island. The Sunderland then continued on to Seal Lake, approximately 700 miles from the North Pole, where Barrett put the big flying boat down for a safe landing on an uncharted lake littered with small icebergs. The following month, Wg Cdr Barrett returned to the lake to recover Simpson's party, who now prepared for the main expedition.

The MV *Tottan* was a steel-hulled 540-ton Norwegian sealer that supported several expeditions to Greenland throughout the 1950s. (Via Martyn Chorlton)

Three 201 Squadron Sunderland Mk Vs carry out a precision formation take-off before setting course for Iceland in support of the British North Greenland Expedition. (*Aeroplane*)

Flying the flag in Greenland

For the main expedition commencing in July 1952, not only would a large amount of equipment travel by sea in MV *Tottan*, but also a significant amount would be flown in by the RAF. This time, five Sunderlands from 230 Squadron would take part, once again routing via Reykjavik and then onwards to Young Sound (74° North). From here, the Sunderlands would play a supporting role transporting 150 tons of stores, dogs and passengers further north to the recently named Britannia Lake.

The whole exercise would be one of the toughest ever taken on by 230 Squadron and under the command of Sqn Ldr Higgins a detachment of 40 aircrew and 20 ground personnel began to prepare for the tough climate.

On the morning of 21 July, the first Sunderland left Pembroke Dock, arriving at Reykjavik in the afternoon. The plan was then to survey the route north to Young Sound, looking for ice en route, which could disrupt the *Tottan*'s journey. With the best intentions, poor weather had stopped Higgins from surveying the route until 28 July, although the aircraft had made it as far as 74° North, but only at 8,000ft, a few hundred feet above icing clouds, forcing the flying boat back to Reykjavik.

By this time, MV *Tottan* had already made it safely through to Young Sound and, on 30 July, sent a signal to Higgins, stating that the landing area was clear of ice and the weather was clear. All five Sunderlands had now arrived at Reykjavik and the same day Higgins, in Sunderland Mk V 'Y' landed at Young Sound at 1715hrs and the RAF ensign was planted in the ground there for the first time. A second Sunderland, 'O', arrived at 2015hrs, having suffered from a troublesome engine en route. Over the next few days, the RAF team set to work preparing a tented camp for the rest of the party. While cold, the work was made easier by 24 hours of daylight and a typical working day lasted from 0600hrs to 2300hrs.

Keen to get on with the task ahead, Higgins, flying 'O' followed by 'Y', left Young Sound, bound for Britannia Lake (the same uncharted lake visited the previous year) on 3 August. Unfortunately, as the first Sunderland arrived over the lake, they found it completely solid with ice, giving the flying boats no option but to return to Young Sound. Cdr Simpson was confident that there would be a sudden change in the weather over the coming days and the RAF contingent prepared the first loads, hopeful that the expedition leader would be right.

In fact, he was proved correct much sooner than expected and, on 5 August, Higgins set out in 'P' for Britannia Lake again, this time finding it completely free of ice. At 1015hrs, Higgins touched down on the five-mile-long, two-mile-wide lake, which was positioned between two giant glaciers, later named Lion and Unicorn. The lake was also flanked by hills that rose to 3,000ft on the northern shore with some smaller hills on the southern one but, other than that, no further problems were foreseen for operating a Sunderland from here at this stage.

The task for those on board the Sunderland was to find a good anchorage point, yet even though the aircraft was taxiing along as close as 50 yards to the shore, no bottom could be found. It was then decided to launch a rubber dinghy instead to explore the shoreline in detail, with Sqn Ldr Higgins, Cdr Simpson, Flt Lt Yates and Flt Lt C. M. Stavert (the deputy OC of 230 Squadron) on board. Once ashore, the small party carried the dinghy overhead for quite some distance before they reached a sandy area where debris had been carried down by the glacier over thousands of years, complete with a shelving bottom. The site was declared perfect for a campsite and an anchorage.

With fresh momentum, a plan was made to begin the airlift to the forward site on 6 August, but a thick fog blew into Young Sound, which scuppered that idea, and, even by 2200hrs, the visibility was still down to just 200 yards. It was not until 7 August that Sqn Ldr Higgins in 'O' took off from Young Sound at 0925hrs, touching down at 1110hrs with Cdr Simpson and his advance party on board. Simpson and the party rowed to shore in a small wooden dinghy specifically designed to be carried on Sunderlands. 'Y' landed at 1335hrs and, using larger rubber dinghies and two expedition dinghies, both aircraft were unloaded. A Saunders-Roe pontoon, used for servicing at Pembroke Dock, was also carried in component form and, under the guidance of Flt Lt W. T. Morrison AFC, was reassembled and aircraft moorings were laid.

230 Squadron Sunderlands moored at Pembroke Dock after arriving back from the second, main expedition in late August 1952. (*Flight* via *Aeroplane*)

Right: Cdr Angus Bruce Erskine RN, who was chosen by Cdr Jim Simpson RN, the leader of the British North Greenland Expedition for his Antarctic experience and ski-mountaineering skills.

Below: A beached 230 Squadron Sunderland at Young Sound in 1953; note the large chunk of ice cruising past in the background. Blocks of ice only a fraction the size of this would make short work of a Sunderland's hull. (*Flight* via *Aeroplane*)

A tricky situation

When Flt Lt Stavert arrived over Britannia Lake on 8 August at 0915hrs, he found that conditions had changed dramatically, with a 35-40kt wind blowing down Unicorn glacier creating 4ft high, white-topped waves. In such conditions, unloading was impossible, and a contingency plan was arranged for a Lancaster ASR.3 (normally based at St Eval – currently on detachment at Reykjavik) to drop an airborne lifeboat into the lake. This was efficiently done at 1317hrs, but, unfortunately, the lifeboat landed nose down in the rough lake, severely damaging the small vessel, including smashing the bows in. Not to be deterred, Cdr Simpson decided to attempt to salvage the lifeboat, accompanied by Lt Erskine and Sgt Shelton-Smith. As the small salvage party proceeded to the scene in a small outboard dinghy, the waves got the better of it and the craft was overturned, forcing all three to swim the final 20 yards in the icy water to the part-sunken lifeboat. Fully aware of what was happening, Flt Lt Stavert had already started the engines of his Sunderland, slipped its moorings and, with great skill, proceeded to taxi towards the wrecked lifeboat. As the Sunderland approached, Cdr Simpson was worried that the aircraft could be damaged and ordered his two colleagues to jump for it. Sgt Shelton-Smith was picked up almost immediately, while Lt Erskine travelled under the hull (keelhauled in navy speak!) of the flying boat before being dragged aboard. Simpson was in a much more dangerous position and passed out of reach. But, once again with great skill, Flt Lt Stavert managed to manoeuvre the flying boat so that Simpson was swept past the forward door. Despite being completely soaked to the core, Sgt Shelton-Smith managed to grab Simpson by the hair and haul him to safety. Incredibly, all three were back at work within three hours of the incident and, despite Flt Lt Stavert's attempt to tow the now upturned lifeboat ashore, he had to cut the craft loose for fear of damaging his aircraft.

On 9 August, the Saunders-Roe pontoon was brought into use, making the task of unloading larger cargo much easier. The loss of the outboard dinghy and airborne lifeboat meant that the pontoon had to be hauled ashore every day, not a pleasant task in a prevailing wind. With the basic infrastructure of the expedition in place, Sunderlands were flown into Britannia Lake at a rate of four or five per day.

All ranks, both RAF and Royal Navy, helping to haul in a Sunderland to the water's edge at Young Sound in August 1953. (Planet News Ltd, *Flight* via *Aeroplane*)

A 201 Squadron Sunderland Mk V moored in front of Tower Bridge for Battle of Britain Week 1953. (Central Press Photos Ltd via *Aeroplane*)

230 Squadron Sunderland Mk V RN270 representing Greenland Operations during Battle of Britain Week in 1953. Transferred to 205/209 Squadron in the Far East, RN270 was SOC on 25 September 1958, one of several to join the 'Kipper Fleet' scrapyard. (*Aeroplane*)

The Ice returns

On 13 August, 'V' lost an outer engine just 20 minutes after leaving Britannia Lake en route to Young Sound. The Sunderland managed to haul itself over the 7,000ft high ice-covered mountains on just three engines and eventually made a safe landing at Young Sound. Following an inspection, it was found that the engine could not be repaired in situ, but if the serviceable inner engine was exchanged for the broken outer then the aircraft could be flown on three to Reykjavik, where a replacement could be fitted. Work began at 1515hrs the following day and, by 0430hrs on 15 August, the engines had been swapped over. While the job sounds straightforward, in the middle of the task, a 60kt gale swept through the camp and caused 'V' to break its moorings. Utterly unfazed by the fact that their aircraft was now cruising down the three-mile wide Young Sound, the engineers continued with their work while Sqn Ldr Higgins and a party of officers set out in a motorboat to attempt to recover the errant flying boat. By now, the Sunderland had picked up a different airstream and was preceding stern-first up the Sound. At last, with the help of lifeboats from MV *Tottan* (which had also broken moorings in the gale), the rearward progress of the Sunderland was brought to a halt just 70 yards from the shore. 'V' was flown out of Young Sound on 18 August by Fg Off E. W. Beer, as planned, direct to Reykjavik.

From this point, the weather began to deteriorate quite rapidly with snow falling on Britannia Lake and fog becoming a problem at Young Sound. On at least three occasions aircraft were forced back to the Sound because the air temperature had dropped to -10° C. From 17 August, ice began to enter Young Sound and, on 19 August, a particularly large section (estimated to be two miles wide) passed close by the aircraft moored there. That same day though, the final flights into Britannia Lake were made, concluding after eight sorties.

On 20 August, a second Sunderland had to depart for Reykjavik on three engines, and the following day saw the final sortie in support of this stage of the expedition. It involved dropping supplies by

201 Squadron Sunderland Mk V SZ567 pictured over the harsh Greenland terrain during the 1953 British North Greenland Expedition resupply operation. Transferred to 230 Squadron via the FBSU in 1954, the Sunderland was scrapped on 15 October 1957. (*Aeroplane*)

parachute for an advance party at Seal Lake, 20 miles west of Britannia Lake and the ice cap. This was something the Sunderland was not designed to do and not every chute opened successfully.

It was 22 August when the last three Sunderlands left Young Sound, bound for Reykjavik. It was not a straightforward departure for any of them with ice all around and fog descending in patches, giving a visibility of between 600 and 1,000 yards. The only safe method of taking off was to taxi along an ice-free path, turnabout, set the compass and take-off into the fog, missing icebergs large and small by mere feet. All three Sunderlands left Young Sound safely, arriving at Reykjavik between 1700 and 1900hrs. By 23 August 1952, all of the aircraft had arrived back at Pembroke Dock, having successfully delivered the British North Greenland Expedition, complete with 250 tons of equipment.

Further tasking

During 1953, the Sunderlands returned to Greenland again, delivering a further 130 tons of stores and equipment, enough to keep the expedition going for another year. Five more Sunderlands of 230 Squadron hit the headlines in August 1954 when they helped bring the expedition home – including a large team of huskies – concluding one of the most challenging peacetime RAF operations ever carried out.

THE RAF AND THE NORTH GREENLAND EXPEDITION 1954 – 'May I take over when we get airborne?', this Greenland husky seems to be saying to the pilot of a 230 Squadron Sunderland flying boat as, in the second pilot's seat, he awaits the aircraft's departure from Young Sound for Pembroke Dock, South Wales. The Sunderland was one of five RAF flying boats which flew home the members of the British North Greenland Expedition from Britannia Lake and Young Sound, with their stores and some of their dogs. (British Official Photograph, *Flight* via *Aeroplane*)

Above and Right:
230 Squadron in neat formation for the camera during a flypast over Pembroke Deck, following the successful conclusion of the British North Greenland Expedition. (*Flight* via *Aeroplane*)

Chapter 10

New Zealand's Queen of the Skies

D espite being formed back in 1923, many RNZAF personnel continued to serve with the
RAF until the late 1940s. Quite a proportion of them served on flying boats with the
RAF, including the Short Sunderland, but it was not until early 1943 that the RNZAF
gained its own flying boat unit.

Mk V NZ4111 of 5 Squadron RNZAF after hitting a submerged rock at Te Whanga Lagoon on November 3, 1959.

Release the 'Taniwha'

Still affiliated to the RAF, 490 (NZ) Squadron was formed on 28 March 1943 at Jui near Freetown (now Sierra Leone), West Africa. Its motto was 'Taniwha kei runga' ('The Taniwha is in the air'). The Taniwha, according to Māori folktale, was a mythical monster that could take on many forms. It was generally associated with water, although a tenuous link with dragons gave the squadron the opportunity to use the creature in their motto.

Under the command of Wg Cdr D. W. Baird DFC, the unit's first aircraft was the Consolidated Catalina Mk IB, an ideal aircraft for operating over the vast mid-Atlantic Ocean, although the Gulf of Guinea was the focus for most operations. Tasked with flying convoy escort, maritime, transport and ASR (Air-Sea Rescue) patrols, 490 Squadron's first operation, a convoy escort, was flown in May 1943. By August, the first of many seamen had been rescued and the same month a U-boat was claimed as damaged.

In December 1943, Wg Cdr Baird made way for Wg Cdr B. S. Nicholl and, in May 1944, the first of several Sunderland Mk IIIs began to arrive on the unit (its Catalinas were retained until July). The first Sunderland operation was flown on 17 May by Flt Lt R. C. Dunn in ML850. The task was an eight-and-a-half hour anti-submarine patrol. This was a typically long and monotonous operation flown by the 490 Squadron crews, described by Wg Cdr Nicholls in the terms of sport: 'This game is rather like cricket. The runs saved in the field count just as much towards winning the game as the runs made off the bat'. New aircraft began to arrive throughout May and June until, eventually, 14 Sunderlands were on charge by the end of the war.

The squadron spent its entire existence operating from Jui, which must have been a very nice posting, especially for the ground engineers and support personnel. However, it also carried several detachments including Stranraer, Fishermans Lake (Liberia), Apapa (Nigeria), Adidjan (Ivory Coast) and Bathhurst/Half Die (Gambia).

Encounters with the enemy were rare and accidents even rarer, with just one Sunderland being lost during service with 490 Squadron. On 14 July 1944, Fg Off M. E. McGreal was at the controls of ML852 whilst flying a routine patrol. He was over 200 miles from shore when the Sunderland's two port engines cut out. McGreal had no option but to ditch off Cape St Mary, West Africa, in a heavy swell. A good landing was carried out but, despite the dinghies being launched very quickly, the aircraft began to break up. Unfortunately, the wireless operator, WO A. P. Opie (last seen sending distress signals) and the flight engineer, Sgt Scott, went down with the aircraft. In the water, injured Welshman Flt Sgt D. C. Jones helped to support another stricken crewman while McGreal inflated a second dinghy. The crew drifted in the open sea, without food or water, until the following evening when rescue finally came from an RAF HSL (High Speed Launch), No. 2523 of 201 ASR Unit.

By October 1944, the squadron was under the charge of its third and final commanding officer, Wg Cdr T. F. Gill. The squadron flew its last operational sortie of World War Two on 6 May 1945 but was shortlisted to take part in the continued fight against Japan. When this did not come about, it was clear that 490 Squadron was surplus to requirements and disbandment beckoned. From July 1943 to May 1945, the squadron flew 463 operational sorties over 4,853 flying hours. While obviously not seeing as much action as other New Zealand units, 490 Squadron certainly played its part by covering an important sector of the Atlantic Ocean. Only nine merchant ships were recorded as being lost in the Gulf of Guinea from September 1943 through to May 1944. 490 (NZ) Squadron was given full credit for helping to protect shipping in the area, especially as no merchant vessels were lost to U-boats post-May 1944 until the end of the war.

On 21 June 1945, those Sunderland Mk IIIs still serving with the squadron were SOC, and on 30 June, the unit was disbanded. Prior to this, in December 1944, four Sunderland Mk IIIs from the squadron (ML792, ML793, ML794 and ML795) led by Wg Cdr D. W. Baird and crewed by tour-expired New Zealand crew, set course for home via Brazil, Texas and through the Pacific. On arrival the four Sunderlands were officially taken on charge by the RNZAF and given new serials: NZ4101, NZ4102, NZ4103 and NZ4104, respectively. All of the flying boats were used to complement the existing air transport services between New Zealand, Noumea, Espiritu Santo and Lauthala Bay in Fiji. All would eventually continue to serve with New Zealand National Airways, re-registered as ZK-AMJ, ZK-AMF, ZK-AMG and ZK-AMK.

Short Sunderland Flying Boats Handed Over To New Zealand Government May 18, 1953 – Mr E B Corbett, Minster of Lands and Maori Affairs, received, on behalf of the New Zealand Government today, from Rear Admiral M S Slattery, at Rochester – the log book of the first of sixteen Short Sunderland flying boats being delivered to the Royal New Zealand Air Force for service in the South Pacific. (Keystone Photo and Caption, via *Aeroplane*)

Ex-VB883 Mk V NZ4107 wearing its final code 'D' before being declared surplus in May 1967. By August, the Sunderland was scrapped at Hobsonville.

NZ4101 *Tainui* on the step at Hobsonville in 1945. The Sunderland Mk III had a short career in New Zealand and, following a short spell with NZNAC (New Zealand National Airways Corporation), the flying boat was scrapped by 1950.

The New Zealand post-war flying boats

By 1952, the RNZAF's Catalinas had served for almost a decade. Their replacements were 16 Sunderland Mk Vs ordered from Short Brothers, all of which were ex-RAF but fully reconditioned. The aircraft were PP110, RN280, VB883, ML814, DP191, PP129, VB880, VB881, PP124, SZ561, SZ584, EJ167, RN286, RN306, PP143 and RN291, and were re-serialled for the RNZAF as NZ4105–NZ4120. All were initially allocated to 5 Squadron RNZAF at Lauthala Bay, Fiji, and 6 Squadron RNZAF stationed at Hobsonville. 6 Squadron's association with the Sunderland was to be short-lived and the unit was replaced by the Maritime Operational Conversion Unit (MOCU). This left 5 Squadron as the RNZAF's main Sunderland operator from 1953 to 1967.

The Sunderlands served the RNZAF with great distinction and, despite endless difficulties with regard to maintenance and flying conditions, only one aircraft was lost in a flying accident. This occurred on 15 April 1961 when NZ4117 'T' had to force-land in heavy seas, without injury to the crew. The aircraft was later beached at Lauthala Bay and scrapped.

Those who lived on the many remote islands in the Pacific during this time have warm memories of the Sunderlands, referring to them as the big white 'flying canoes'. The flying boats would often be the only lifeline to the islands, delivering medical supplies, passengers and freight to places where conventional aircraft could not go. Sunderlands would often land on unlit lagoons, at great risk to man and machine, to evacuate ill patients to hospital in a matter of hours, compared to travelling by boat, which could take days.

By April 1962, 5 Squadron's strength was reduced from six Sunderlands to four and all servicing facilities were transferred to Hobsonville where the MOCU had its three aircraft as well. The MOCU was re-titled the Maritime Reconnaissance & Support Unit (MRSU) not long after but was disbanded by February 1965. At the same time, 5 Squadron was withdrawn from Lauthala Bay to move as a whole to Hobsonville, leaving behind a detachment of two Sunderlands at Fiji for routine commitments. In October 1965, conversion training for the Sunderland ceased and the detachment at Fiji was reduced to a single aircraft. NZ4107 'D' flew the last RNZAF Sunderland sortie on 2 April 1967 when it was flown back to Hobsonville following the closure of Lauthala two days earlier.

This final flight signalled the end of almost 30 years of continuous Sunderland military service. NZ4108 was already operating in 'Civvie Street' as VH-BRF with Ansett airlines. NZ4115 'Q' was also saved from the axe after it was presented to the Museum of Transport and Technology (MOTAT) in Auckland on 12 December 1966.

NZ4120 of 5 Squadron RNZAF pictured over the Philippine Sea in 1959.

Sunderland Mk III NZ4103 *Mataatua* getting airborne at Hobsonville in 1945 whilst serving with 1 Aircraft Depot. After brief service with the NZNAC, the aircraft returned to the RNZAF but, after being put up for sale at least twice, the flying boat was scrapped in early 1955.

RNZAF Sunderland histories

NZ4101: c/n 4668, Mk III, ex-ML792. Sent to 302 Ferry Training Unit (FTU), Oban (Wg Cdr Baird) 18 October 1944; to 1 Aircraft Depot, Hobsonville, 4 December 1944; named *Tainui*; SOC 16 December 1947; sold to New Zealand National Airways Corporation (NZNAC); sold by tender 10 October 1949 and disposed of by 10 November 1949; it was later scrapped.

NZ4102: c/n 4666, Mk III, ex-ML793. Sent to 302 FTU, Oban (Flt Lt Patience) 23 October 1944; to 1 Aircraft Depot, Hobsonville, 4 December 1944; named *Tokomaru*; converted by RNZAF for passengers in November 1946; SOC 30 September 1947; sold to NZNAC and registered as ZK-AMF; only used as standby, aircraft and registration were cancelled on 2 December 1947; believed to have been traded back to the RNZAF for NZ4104 and returned to military service on 9 February 1951; offered for sale on 28 May 1951, but unsold; surplus by November 1954 and put up for sale again on 2 May 1955; sold to NZ Metal Smelters Ltd for £350 and scrapped.

NZ4103: c/n 4667, Mk III, ex-ML794. Sent to 302 FTU, Oban (Flt Lt Shepherd) 18 October 1944; to 1 Aircraft Depot, Hobsonville, 4 December 1944; named *Mataatua*; SOC 30 September 1947; sold to NZNAC and registered ZK-AMG until 31 March 1949; returned to RNZAF 9 February 1951; offered for sale by tender on 28 May 1951 but unsold; offered for sale again on 23 November 1953; unsold again and declared surplus 3 November 1954; scrapped.

NZ4104: c/n 4668, Mk III; ex-ML795. Sent to 302 FTU, Oban (Flt Lt Pettit) 27 October 1944; to 1 Aircraft Depot, Hobsonville, 4 December 1944; named *Takitimu;* SOC 16 December 1947; sold to NZNAC and registered ZK-AMK; converted to carry passengers in 1948 and entered service with NZNAC in Mar 1949; flew the last NZNAC Sunderland service from Suva to Auckland on 31 May 1950; returned to RNZAF 9 February 1951; offered for sale by tender 28 May 1951 but unsold; transferred to 6 Squadron RNZAF at Hobsonville, May 1952; offered for sale by tender 23 November 1953 but unsold again and declared surplus 3 November 1954; scrapped.

NZ4105: Mk V, ex-PP110. Brought on Charge (BOC) at Fiji 13 June 1953 at a cost of £61,500 (the Mk Vs from NZ4105 to NZ4120 cost this sum to BOC) and delivered to 5 Squadron RNZAF at Lauthala Bay in August 1953; displayed codes 'KN-A', 'KN-C' and 'A'; from 1958 in store at Hobsonville; SOC 2 August 1966 and sold; scrapped at Hobsonville, August 1967.

NZ4106: Mk V, ex-RN280. BOC at Hobsonville 24 April 1954; displayed 'KN-G', 'KN-B' and 'B'; served with 6 Squadron RNZAF at Hobsonville from 27 April to 18 May 1954; SOC at Lauthala Bay on 20 March 1962 and declared surplus; written off at Hobsonville on 2 October 1962 and reduced to spares; remains sold 11 January 1963.

NZ4107: Mk V, ex-VB883. BOC at Hobsonville 22 September 1954; displayed codes 'XX-C', 'XX-D', 'KN-F' and 'D'; flew final RNZAF Sunderland flight from Lauthala Bay to Hobsonville on 2 April 1967; declared surplus 3 May 1967 and SOC; sold to Australian Aircraft Sales in August 1967; scrapped at Hobsonville.

NZ4108: Mk V, ex-ML814. BOC at Fiji 13 June 1953; delivered to 5 Squadron RNZAF, Lauthala Bay by August 1953; displayed codes 'KN'B' and 'XX-D'; to MOCU, Hobsonville, 4 January to 20 August 1956; SOC 12 December 1963 as surplus and sold to Airlines of New South Wales as VH-BRF; entered service with Airlines of New South Wales in August 1964 after refurbishment; to Antilles Air Boats, Virgin Islands, as N158J in 1974; to Edward Hulton in 1979 as G-BJHS; to Kermit Weeks in 1992 and re-registered N158J; registered N814ML 16 September 1993; extant.

NZ4109: Mk V, ex-DP191. BOC at Fiji 21 July 1953; displayed code 'KN-C'; stored at Hobsonville by 1962 and SOC there in February 1965; sold to Ingot Metals, Auckland, for £15; scrapped at Hobsonville, 1965–66.

NZ4110: Mk V, ex-PP129. BOC at Fiji 5 October 1953; displayed code 'KN-F'; stored at Hobsonville from 1956 and converted to instructional airframe 'INST183' on 14 October 1959 with TTS, Hobsonville; became the first of the 16 Mk Vs to be SOC at Hobsonville 14 April 1964; scrapped at Hobsonville, 1964–65.

NZ4111: Mk V, ex-VB880. BOC at Fiji 6 September 1953; test flown from Lauthala Bay by Wg Cdr B. LePine on 14 September 1953; displayed codes 'KN'D', 'XX-B', 'XX-K' and 'K'; with 5 Squadron

RNZAF 6 March to 11 April 1959 as 'KN-D'; part of flypast to mark opening of Auckland Harbour Bridge 30 May 1959; damaged in taxiing accident in Chatham Islands when the aircraft struck rocks in Te Whanga Lagoon and sank in shallow water, 4 November 1959; all usable components removed and aircraft written off on 9 December 1959; the fuselage was later removed from the water by a local farmer and sections used for storage.

NZ4112: Mk V, ex-VB881. BOC at Hobsonville 2 November 1953; to 5 Squadron, RNZAF, displaying codes 'KN-A', 'KN-L' and 'L'; SOC 2 August 1966 and sold to Australian Aircraft Sales; fuselage used by Hobsonville Yacht Club until 1970; cockpit and forward fuselage (mainly the front turret area) was saved and moved to Ferrymead Museum, Christchurch, by an RNZAF Hercules; remainder of aircraft scrapped; parts extant.

NZ4113: Mk V, ex-PP124. BOC at Hobsonville 7 August 1954; displayed codes 'KN-D', 'KN-M', 'XX-D' and 'M'; to 6 Squadron, RNZAF, Hobsonville, from 15 February 1955 to 23 March 1956; to MOCU, Hobsonville, from 21 May 1956 to 17 October 1957; famously scraped keel along runway during the official opening of Rongotai on 25 October 1959 after being caught in a downdraft; returned to Hobsonville and beached for repairs; flew last RNZAF Sunderland service to Chatham Islands on 22 March 1967; declared surplus 3 May 1967 and sold to Australian Aircraft Sales in August; scrapped at Hobsonville.

NZ4114: c/n SH.1473b, Mk V, ex-SZ561. BOC at Hobsonville 2 August 1954; displayed codes 'XX-A' and 'P'; to MOCU May 1955 to 25 June 1956; to 5 Squadron RNZAF; SOC 6 February 1967 and sold to Australian Aircraft Sales; stripped and fuselage given to Northland Coastguard for use as an HQ; towed to Whangarei and beached at Onerahi 11 July 1967; sold 1972 and scrapped.

NZ4115: c/n SH.1552b, Mk V, ex-SZ584 and G-AHJR. BOC at Hobsonville 17 November 1953; to 5 Squadron RNZAF and displayed codes 'KN-A', 'KN-B', 'KN-Q' and 'Q'; SOC 9 December 1966 and presented to MOTAT on 22 December 1966; extant.

NZ4116: c/n SH.818b, Mk V, ex-EJ167. BOC at Hobsonville 27 July 1953; displayed codes 'KN-C', 'KN-G', 'KN-S' and 'S'; SOC 6 February 1967 and sold to Australian Aircraft Sales; scrapped at Hobsonville.

NZ4117 Mk V, ex-RN286. BOC at Hobsonville 9 May 1953; displayed codes 'KN-K', 'KN-T' and 'T'; damaged at Tarawa, 15 April 1961 when force-landed in rough seas; returned to Lauthala Bay and beached for salvage; written off 10 August 1961 and scrapped at Lauthala Bay.

NZ4118: Mk V, ex-RN306. BOC at Hobsonville 13 May 1954; displayed code 'XX-A'; to 6 Squadron RNZAF, Hobsonville, from 18 May 1954 to 14 December 1955; to MOCU, Hobsonville, from 7 March 1956 to 11 October 1957; in store at Hobsonville from 1960; written off in 1965 and sold to Ingot Metals, Auckland, for £15; scrapped at Hobsonville, 1965–66.

NZ4119: Mk V, ex-PP143. BOC at Hobsonville 22 April 1954; displayed code 'XX-B'; to 6 Squadron RNZAF from 27 April 1954 to 23 September 1955; to MOCU, Hobsonville, from 25 November 1955 to 9 August 1957; in store at Hobsonville from 1960; declared surplus 20 March 1962 and written off as spares 2 October 1962.

NZ4120: Mk V, ex-RN291. BOC at Hobsonville 6 May 1954; to 6 Squadron RNZAF until 3 September 1957; moved to Hobsonville from Lauthala Bay; to 5 Squadron RNZAF; displayed codes 'XX-C', 'KN-Z' and 'Z'; in store at Hobsonville from 1965; SOC 2 August 1966 and sold by tender; scrapped at Hobsonville, December 1966–January 1967.

Mk V NZ4111 of 5 Squadron RNZAF after hitting a submerged rock at Te Whanga Lagoon on 3 November 1959.

Mk V NZ4112 'L' during a visit to Seletar on 23 May 1965. (Via Martyn Chorlton)

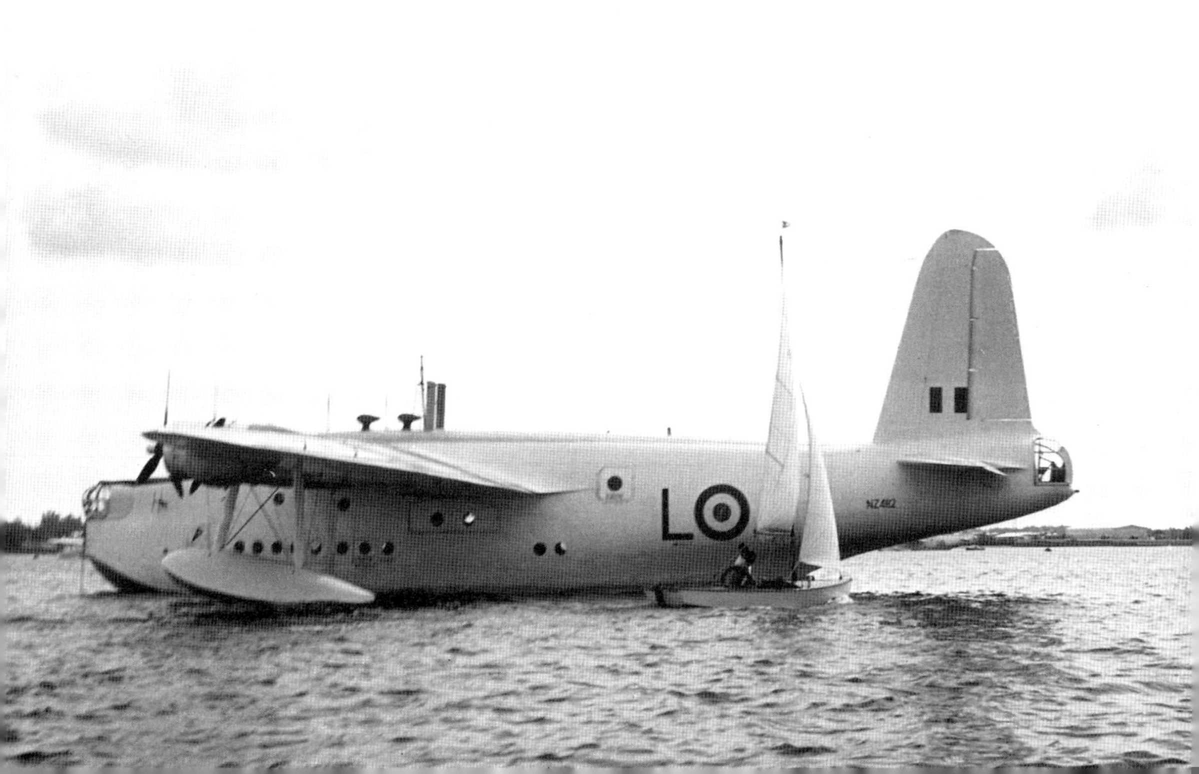

NZ4112 again, this time at Hobsonville in 1964. The aircraft served solely with 5 Squadron RNZAF from 1953 to 1966, later being used by the Hobsonville Yacht Club.

NZ4120 settles heavily in the water after landing at Lauthala Bay in 1960. The flying boat was placed in storage at Hobsonville in 1965, SOC in 1966 and was scrapped by early 1967.

The final RNZAF Sunderland flypast over Lauthala Bay, Fiji, in November 1964, before all examples of the flying boat were regrouped at Hobsonville. (*Aeroplane*)

'Somewhere in the South Pacific'. Sunderland Mk V (ex-VB880) pictured on 30 August 1953 only days before it was officially BOC (Brought on Charge) in Fiji. It is believed that this photograph shows the flying boat being used during a beaching exercise for future RNZAF ground personnel. The flying boat is already displaying 5 Squadron RNZAF code 'KN'. (Via *Aeroplane*)

Chapter 11

Civil Sisters

Imperial to BOAC

The rapid expansion of the Empire air routes in the late 1930s led Imperial Airways to order a new fleet of flying boats capable of carrying both passengers and mail to the far-flung corners of the Empire.

The C-Class flying boats could operate in areas with few facilities and, from 1937, were providing a regular service to South Africa, east to India and on to Australia, in partnership with Qantas.

The order from Imperial Airways was the largest Short Brothers had seen. The aircraft were built alongside the new Sunderland, and larger transatlantic G-Class flying boats followed. Even a large civil landplane was starting construction when the war intervened.

The Ministry of Aircraft Production demanded that Short Brothers concentrate Seaplane Works' efforts on the Sunderland and, at the end of April 1940, *Clifton* and *Cleopatra* were the last two C-Class boats to be launched. Another, part way through construction, was abandoned – its parts and the C-Class jigs and tools were recycled into the war effort.

The newly formed BOAC, formed in April 1940, took over Imperial's fleet, but with the inevitable losses of some aircraft, began to urgently need more flying boats. Without the tooling to build more C- or G-Class flying boats, the Sunderland was seen as a possible stopgap option.

The first batch of six converted Sunderlands, JM660–JM665, was ordered for BOAC in 1942. They were spartan inside, compared to the pre-war luxury of the Empire flying boats. The turret openings were covered with fairings, and bench and mattress seating provided basic accommodation. Standard camouflage was used but with large civil registrations underlined with red, white and blue stripes. The aircraft were initially operated on the Poole to West Africa route from January 1943. In August, a further five (ML725–ML729) were converted. The civil Sunderlands were then used on the Poole–Karachi route via Cairo, eventually extending to Calcutta. Obviously, they took the longer route via Gibraltar until the liberation of France enabled direct routes to be used again. The aircraft operating through the military areas of North Africa wore military markings. The first 11 were followed with 12 more before the war's end: ML751–ML756 and ML786–ML791.

Two of the civil Sunderlands met with accidents: G-AGES crashed in Ireland in July 1943, killing ten on board and injuring another 15. In November of the same year, G-AGIB crashed in the desert at night near Tobruk, killing all 19 on board.

Post-war, BOAC refitted the remaining aircraft with proper passenger interiors and bigger windows. ML754 was the first to be modified and was subsequently redesignated G-AGJM *Hythe* – the name adopted for the new class of converted Sunderlands. There were three different interiors on the Hythes: The H1 had 16 seats with sleeping berths, the H2 introduced a Promenade Deck and the H3 had 22 seats.

Planning to reopen the Empire routes, BOAC started a service between Britain and Singapore in January 1946, eventually sending G-AGJM *Hythe* on a survey of routes to Australia, New Zealand, Hong Kong and further afield. The 'Dragon' route operated to Hong Kong where 88 Squadron carried out a courier service to Japan for the occupation forces. The Sydney service was shared with Qantas and commenced in May 1946, with a typical journey time of five and a half days.

The Hythes began to be phased out by BOAC towards the end of 1948 – with Lockheed Constellations operating a parallel service – until the last Hythe left Rose Bay in Sydney in February 1949. It was not the end of the fleet though – a fledgling Aquila Airways saw an opportunity to make use of the flying boats in the Berlin Airlift and eventually on scheduled services.

Above: Ex-Mk III EJ156, which served with 423 Squadron during the war, was given a new role as G-AGWW with RAF Transport Command, and then as CX-AFA with CAUSA (Compañía Aeronáutica Uruguaya S.A.) from 1947. (Via Martyn Chorlton)

Right: The first of six Sunderlands ordered by BOAC was ex-JM660, which became G-AGER *Hatfield* in January 1943. (Via Martyn Chorlton)

Sunderland ex-ML725 wearing the Transport Command code OQZC. Transferred to BOAC as G-AGHW, the aircraft came to grief on the Isle of Wight in November 1947. (Via Martyn Chorlton)

Above: The first 'proper' civilian Sunderland conversion was ex-ML754; the first of the Hythe-Class flying boats. (Via Martyn Chorlton)

Left: Conversion of a Sunderland to a Sandringham, showing the new nose section being installed. The nose frames have been modified to give a more streamlined form, reminiscent of the Empire flying boats. (Via Allan King)

The new streamlined tail section of the Sandringham being attached to the main fuselage. This aircraft was to become G-AGPZ, the first Sandringham 2 sold to Dodero in Argentina. (Via Allan King)

The Sandringham

Meanwhile, Short Brothers had been working on a replacement design that would combine elements of the Empire Boat with the Sunderland. G-AGKX (formerly ML788) was returned to the factory to be fitted with a new streamlined nose and tail and given a refurbished luxury interior on two decks. The new design was the Short Sandringham I, relaunched in November 1945 for brief trials with the RAF as OQZF. Short Brothers were bringing luxury back into flying again; the Sandringham I could accommodate 24 day passengers in comfort with dining facilities, a cocktail bar and features such as a ladies' 'powder room', dressing rooms and points for electric razors. Space for mail and other cargo were provided in the nose and rear fuselage.

It was, however, an interim design – landplane alternatives were being developed hurriedly, if not well. Short Brothers also had hopes for a civil development of the larger Short Shetland as an airliner. Following much lobbying by Saunders-Roe, the Ministry of Supply had added large flying boats to the lists produced by the Brabazon Committee, but BOAC only ever saw flying boats as a short-term post-war solution.

However, BOAC would not be the first customer. Instead, interest came from overseas and the Sandringham designs were dictated by the needs of the airlines and the routes they were flying.

The first commercial version, the Sandringham 2, was created to meet the requirement of an order from Argentinean shipping magnate Señor Dodero. His airline wanted Sandringhams built with Pratt & Whitney Twin Wasp engines to operate along the River Plate. The Sandringham 2 was to be used on a relatively short route, so the interior was rearranged to accommodate 45 passengers – 28 on the lower deck and seating for another 17 and a cocktail bar on the upper deck. The Dodero order was soon followed by another for two Sandringham 3s, which were used on the longer routes along the Paraguay River and had seating for just 21 passengers on the lower deck but with a dining saloon and cocktail bar above.

Also operating on the River Plate was CAUSA (Compañía Aeronáutica Uruguaya S.A.) in Uruguay, which wanted Sandringhams that could accommodate either 40 or 45 passengers but could not afford the more expensive conversion. Instead, CAUSA opted for three simpler one-deck conversions without the Sandringham nose and tail. Two of these were Pegasus-engined Sunderland Mk IIIs; the other was a Sunderland Mk V with the American engines.

The Dodero flying boats were transferred to ALFA (Avacion Litoral Fluvial Argentino) and later, with the creation of Aerolineas Argentinas in 1950, the remaining flying boats were again transferred. They operated in competition with CAUSA's civil Sunderlands, and both fleets had lengthy careers operating with both passengers and on cargo flights until they were taken out of service in the early 1960s.

The Sandringham 4 was designed for 30 passengers to meet an order for four aircraft from TEAL (Tasman Empire Airways Ltd) in New Zealand. They were used on the Auckland to Sydney route that had been maintained by two ageing Empire Boats. Also in New Zealand were four RNZAF Sunderland Mk IIIs, NZ4101–4104, which had been used between Auckland and Fiji – the service being taken over by the domestic airline New Zealand National Airways.

TEAL was, however, not happy with the Sandringham, after one aircraft suffered an engine overheating problem and had to jettison all the baggage from the flight. Concerns about the Twin Wasps overheating led TEAL to operate the Solent (with its larger weight carrying capacity) instead.

BOAC's next order was for nine Plymouth Class Sandringham 5s – a single deck configuration for 22 day, or 16 night, passengers. All were converted from little-used Mk Vs with Twin Wasp engines. They were put into service on the Poole–Sydney and Hong Kong routes and soon after to Iwakuni in Japan. In early 1948, the Plymouth Class was succeeded by three more Sandringham 7s – the Bermuda Class, with accommodation for 30 passengers – for the Far East routes. The BOAC flying boats travelled over

Displaying the short-lived Transport Command registration of OQZF during trials, ex-ML788 was the prototype Sandringham I. The aircraft later served with Aquila Airways before being withdrawn in March 1953 and scrapped at Hamble in August 1953. (Via Martyn Chorlton)

Left: G-AGPZ had a busy wartime career as a Sunderland Mk III before being converted to a Sandringham 2 in 1945. The flying boat was sold to Dodero as LV-AAP *Argentina* but crashed at Buenos Aires on 29 July 1948. (Via Martyn Chorlton)

Below: TEAL (Tasman Empire Airways Limited) Sandringham 4 ZK-AME *New Zealand* on the step in 1946. (Via Martyn Chorlton)

25 million miles, but in November 1950, all flying boat activities ceased, when the airline turned to solely land-based operations. Many of BOAC's remaining aircraft were acquired by Aquila Airways.

The Sandringham 6 was built for an order placed by Norwegian Air Lines (DNL) to operate flying boats along the Norwegian coast between Oslo and Tromsø. Three Sandringhams could carry 37 day passengers on two decks. A unique feature of these aircraft was retention of the ASV radar installation, which proved essential for navigating the coastline of Norway. All three aircraft were lost in accidents and were replaced by two more, but services stopped after DNL was merged with Scandinavian Air Services in 1951.

Seaford to Solent

With the Sunderland proving itself a useful basis for a civilian conversion, there was an almost inevitable eye cast towards the Short Seaford (formerly Sunderland Mk IV) with its Bristol Hercules engines and larger weight carrying capacity for similar conversion. The first request was made by BOAC in December 1945, with the hope that the first aircraft would be available by July the following year.

Short Seaford NJ201 was converted to passenger-carrying G-AGWU in a similar manner to the Sandringham, with the streamlined nose and tail and a twin deck interior cabin. The aircraft was named Solent I and loaned to BOAC for evaluation. BOAC preferred a different layout and the first aircraft it ordered was the new-build Solent 2, with 34 seats arranged over two decks and a large cargo door on the rear of the port side.

BOAC had already decided to phase out its flying boat operations, planning to replace the Hythes on the Australian service with Avro Tudor IIs. With the Solents expected to be replaced within two years, the Treasury agreed to the relatively new Ministry of Civil Aviation (MCA) buying the Solents to be leased to the airline.

The first of the 12 new Solent 2s was G-AHIL, named *Salisbury*, which was launched in November 1946, entering service in May 1948. The last of the new build Solent 2s was G-AHIY *Southsea*, which had the distinction of being the last aircraft built at Short Brothers Seaplane Works on the Medway at Rochester. With the Plymouth Class Sandringhams on the Far East routes, the Solents were destined for Africa.

Within a couple of months, all the Solents were grounded and withdrawn from service after a number of serious faults were found. Propellers were changed for heavier types, engines were modified and the wing tip floats – which had insufficient water clearance at take-off – were moved outwards and slightly forwards and mounted on two pairs in inclined struts. There were also other modifications to deal with, such as eliminating vibrations between the wings and fuselage. These were not approved until September, when the aircraft were able to resume their services.

BOAC, realising it needed six more aircraft, then requested the conversion of six Seafords that had been declared redundant by the RAF. Converted to Solent 3s in Belfast, they offered space for 39 passengers by extending the upper deck into the rear cargo compartment and entered BOAC service a year later.

The Solent's life with BOAC was very short-lived and, by November 1950, it had been replaced by the Handley Page Hermes 4 and the fleet was returned to the MCA. This caused the Ministry a financial headache when the worldwide market for large flying boats was found to be very limited and it was unable to sell more than a handful of the aircraft.

BOAC's decision pre-empted the completion of the last two Solent 3s (G-AKNT and G-AKNU), which, due to production delays both at Short and Harland in Belfast and also with the Bristol Engine Company, were never delivered. Aquila benefitted from the deal, buying G-AKNU cheaply and operating it as *Sydney* for many years.

There were only four more Solents built, all ordered by TEAL under the designation Solent 4 to supersede its Sandringham 4s. They were well furnished for 44 passengers and, with Hercules 733 engines cleared to operate up to 81,000lb weight, they had a range of 3,000 miles. The Solent 4s operated between New Zealand and Tahiti, Fiji, Suva and the Cook Islands, until the final route, Fiji–Tahiti, ceased in September 1960.

Left: 'Orange, Sir?' Aquila Airways maintained the high quality of service that passengers on flying boats had come to expect since the 1930s. This photo was taken on board G-AGEU *R.M.A. Hampshire* whilst on the Southampton–Lisbon–Madeira route. (Aquila Airways via Allan King)

Below: Norwegian Air Lines (DNL) Sandringham 6 LN-IAV (ex-ML809) *Kvithjorn*. The aircraft was lost on 28 August 1947, when, in heavy fog, the flying boat hit a mountain near Lødingsfjellet, Hinnoy, killing all seven crew and 28 passengers on board.

Above: Originally built as a Seaford Mk I, NJ201 was converted into the first Solent I, serving with BOAC as G-AGWU *City of Funchal*. (Via Martyn Chorlton)

Right: Solent 2 G-AHIN *Southampton* appropriately in the seaplane dock at Berth 50, Southampton, unloading baggage. (BOAC via Allan King)

The Twilight Period

Australia had a long connection to flying boat operations as part of the Empire routes, but other domestic flying boat services began in 1947 when Trans Oceanic Airways had acquired some ex-RAAF Sunderlands and operated services from Sydney to Lord Howe Island, the Solomons and the New Hebrides. When TEAL sold its Sandringhams in December 1949, the Sydney-based Ansett Airways took over the aircraft and, from 1953, the airline operated the route to Lord Howe Island, halfway between Australia and New Zealand.

But it was the twilight period for flying boats, as land aircraft took over more and more routes leaving only a few specialised destinations, like Lord Howe Island and the River Plate routes.

Sir Gordon Taylor acquired Bermuda Class Sandringham 7 G-AKCO *St George* and operated charter cruises around New Guinea. It was sold to Reseau Aerien Interinsulaire and re-registered F-OBIP. It was in use until the mid-1960s.

In San Francisco, South Pacific Airlines acquired three redundant Solents for use on a new trans-Pacific service. It had planned a refuelling stop at Christmas Island, but nuclear testing put paid to those plans and the Solents languished, unused.

In the UK, the new airline, Aquila Airways, came into being in 1948, founded by ex-RAF flying boat pilot Barry Aikman to exploit just the type of specialist services flying boats were still ideal for.

Initially, Aquila operated three Hythes, which were quickly put into service as part of the Berlin airlift. Aquila then acquired more Hythes from BOAC (many for spares) and started new scheduled flights from Southampton to Madeira and Funchal, under an associate agreement with British European Airways. Trooping contracts and charter flights supplemented the scheduled services and destinations included Lisbon, Jersey, Marseilles and Capri.

The longest charter was a remarkable trip from Southampton to the Falklands and back in 1952. Routes were explored for flights connecting Southampton, Glasgow and Edinburgh, but these never went ahead.

Aquila operated from the famous Berth 50 at Southampton that had been the starting point for Imperial and BOAC Empire flights. Being the country's only flying boat airline, this of course brought the disadvantages of having to maintain its unique airport. But despite the costs, Aquila continued, later as part of Britavia, and managed to acquire replacement aircraft from BOAC, TEAL and other sources.

The first of 12 new-build Solent 2s was G-AHIL named *Salisbury*. Launched in November 1946, the flying boat was later converted to a Solent 3 and renamed *City of Salisbury*. (Via Martyn Chorlton)

In addition to the relative ease of operating a fleet of similar aircraft, Aquila/Britavia's decision to stay with the Short Brothers-built aircraft may also have been influenced by government policy restricting access to overseas currency for purchasing aircraft not built in the UK. The Madeira route continued until September 1958, when the airline finally ceased operations, marking the end of British commercial flying boat operations.

In Buenos Aires, the Sandringhams and Sunderlands of Aerolineas Argentinas continued working until 1962, when this airline also ceased operating them. They were, however, laid up and the six survivors were preserved until 1967 when they were finally broken up for scrap.

Ansett Airlines continued the longest flying boat service, providing an essential link to Lord Howe Island. In July 1963, one of their aircraft, VH-BRE *Pacific Chieftain*, was wrecked in a storm on Lord Howe Island, leaving the airline with just one flying boat, VH-BRC *Beachcomber*. The RNZAF was persuaded to release one of its remaining Sunderlands, which was converted at Sydney, emerging as a VH-BRF *Islander* in October 1964. It was fitted out for 43 passengers but did not have the full Sandringham nose so is probably best classed as a civil Sunderland.

The two flying boats soldiered on providing a unique scheduled service to Lord Howe Island until 1974, when an airstrip was finally built. Both were sold to Charles Blair's Antilles Air Boats in the Caribbean. Four years later, Charles Blair was killed in a Grumman Goose crash and the two aircraft ended their commercial operations, marking the end of commercial flights by large flying boats.

Beachcomber became the centrepiece of the Solent Sky Museum at Southampton and *Islander* was kept airworthy for some time, until being sold to Kermit Weeks, who flew it out to his Fantasy of Flight museum in Florida. It was the last airworthy Sunderland.

Another ex-Seaford, NJ202 was G-AKNO *Seaforth* (renamed *City of London* soon after), part of a second batch of six converted to Solent 3s for BOAC. (Via Martyn Chorlton)

TEAL Solent 4 ZK-AML (ex-G-AOBL) *R.M.A. Aotearoa II* pictured on 8 December 1949. (Via Martyn Chorlton)

Ex-ML786 Mk III G-AGKV *Huntingdon* pictured during major maintenance in 1946 at Hythe, on the edge of Southampton Water. The aircraft began its service life with Transport Command as OQZD before being converted by Short and Harland. The Sunderland joined BOAC on 12 July 1944 and was not withdrawn until May 1951. (*Aeroplane*)

Chapter 12
The Survivors

Short Sunderland Mk III/Mk V/Sandringham 4
(JM715/ZK-AMH/VH-BRC/N158C – Solent Sky, Southampton

On paper, JM715 was to enter service as a Mk III, part of a 50-strong order received by Short Brothers, Rochester, in 1942. However, after leaving the production line, the aircraft was flown direct to 1 Flying Boat Servicing Unit (FBSU) at Wig Bay on 18 July 1943. On 8 January 1944, JM715 was transferred to 57 MU, also at Wig Bay, and was 'Held in Reserve', destined never to serve with an RAF flying unit. In April 1945, JM715 was brought out of storage and flown to the Flying Boat Modification Unit (FBMU) at Caird's Yard, Greenock, where the aircraft was converted to Mk V standard.

In March 1946, Short Brothers received an order from TEAL for four civilian conversions of the Sunderland, called the Sandringham 4. JM715 was bought back from the Air Ministry on 30 April 1947 and was delivered, possibly from 57 MU direct to Musgrave Channel, for conversion to a Sandringham 4 Tasman Class at the Short Brothers Belfast factory.

Allocated Short's official conversion designation, SH.55C (c/n 2018), the aircraft was registered with TEAL as ZK-AMH on 29 May 1947. TEAL was no stranger to Short-built flying boats, having acquired a pair of S.30 Empire Class in 1940, which it operated until 1947. On 15 October 1947, ZK-AMH began the 12,000-mile journey from Poole Harbour, Dorset, to Waitemata Harbour, Auckland, with Capt H. J. Rose at the controls. The remarkable ferry flight took the Sandringham via Marseilles, Augusta, Cairo, Bahrein, Karachi, Calcutta, Rangoon, Bangkok, Singapore, Sourabaya, Darwin, Bowen and Sydney, arriving in Auckland on 29 October after 87 hours in the air.

ZK-AMH, now named *R.M.A. Auckland*, was pressed into service on 7 November, flying the 1,300-mile Sydney to Auckland route. Engine overheating problems saw the Sandringham fleet grounded from February through to June 1948 following successful rectification work. ZK-AMH's career with TEAL was destined to be short and, in December 1949, the Sandringham was withdrawn from service and stored at Hobsonville, Auckland. On 27 April 1950, ZK-AMH was flown from Auckland to Brisbane for its potential sale to Barrier Reef Airlines by Capt S. Middlemiss. The following day, the Sandringham was sold for £5,000 and, not long after, was fully overhauled and the seating capacity was raised from 30 to 41 passengers.

Reregistered as VH-BRC on 22 May 1950, the aircraft was renamed *Coral Clipper* and began a new service the following day, flying from Brisbane to Lindeman Island, Daydream Island and back to Brisbane. This service was to be short-lived, however, and on 23 January 1951, the Sandringham was withdrawn from use. Briefly removed from the Australian Aircraft Register, the Sandringham was placed in temporary storage pending a full refit, following the sinking of sister machine VH-BRD.

On 15 December 1952, VH-BRC was registered with Ansett Flying boat Service Ltd and was renamed once more, as *Beachcomber*. Services recommenced; this time between Sydney and Brisbane and, in early 1953, the Sandringham began the first of many trips to Lord Howe Island, over 600 miles northeast of Canberra. The Sandringham was destined to become a regular 'lifeline' to the remote island and yet, it was whilst staying overnight at the island that VH-BRC's flying almost came to an end. On 9 June 1974, the Sandringham broke its moorings during a storm and was damaged as it came ashore. Local repairs were carried out and by July it had been ferried to Sydney for more permanent repairs, which were completed by late August.

On 10 September 1974, VH-BRC made the final short flying boat passenger carrying service from Sydney to Lord Howe Island and back. The following day, the Sandringham returned to Lord Howe to collect equipment, having made its 1,360th island flight.

The flying boat was then sold to Antilles Air Boats based in the Virgin Islands and re-registered as N158C. Renamed again as *Southern Star*, by the time it was prepared for delivery to its new owners, it was called *Southern Cross*. On 28 November 1974, with an impressive 17,820 flying hours on the clock, the Sandringham left Sydney for the final time. In March 1976, the aircraft was registered as VP-LVE but, following the death of the company's owner, Capt Charles F. Blair on 2 September 1978, the Sandringham was placed in storage at Grande, Puerto Rico.

Remarkably, the preservation movement had been keeping a close eye on the busy career of this Sandringham and the Science Museum in London was very keen to purchase it. By October 1980, a deal had been struck and the flying boat (now registered as N158C) was restored to a flyable condition in order to make the long flight back to England from San Juan, via St Croix, Boston, Port Washington, Oyster Bay, Sydney (Nova Scotia), Gander and finally Killaloe in Ireland. It was here that the flying boat remained for three months while approval was gained from the Civil Aviation Authority (CAA) to operate the aircraft in UK airspace. On 2 February 1981, the Sandringham arrived at Calshot for storage, by now with 19,500 flying hours under its belt.

Resplendent in its Ansett Flying boat Service Ltd colours, VH-BRC *Beachcomber* takes pride of place in the Hall of Aviation at Southampton, now known as Solent Sky. (Martyn Chorlton)

On 6 July 1981, N158C was moved to HMS Daedalus, Lee-on-Solent, for storage but it was not until 1982 that the Science Museum parted with £85,000 to secure ownership. On 1 March 1983, the Sandringham was moved to Southampton docks for storage and, whilst there, was painted in Antilles colours and re-marked VH-BRC *Beachcomber*. On 27–28 August, the aircraft was installed as the central exhibit of the brand-new Hall of Aviation at Southampton, now known as Solent Sky, which was officially opened on 26 May 1984.

VH-BRC working for a living at Rose Bay, Sydney Harbour, in the early 1970s. (Via Martyn Chorlton)

VH-BRC about to depart Rose Bay bound for Brisbane, 500 miles north of Sydney. (Via Martyn Chorlton)

Above: VH-BRC, after breaking its moorings in a storm, on the beach at Lord Howe Island in 1974. (Via Martyn Chorlton)

Left: N158C became VP-LVE but was destined to spend some time in storage following the death of Antilles Air Boats' owner, Charles Blair. (*Aeroplane*)

Below: By the time VP-LVE was finally retired and displayed at Solent Sky, this venerable flying boat had flown for almost 20,000 hours. (Via Martyn Chorlton)

Short Sunderland Mk III/Mk V/Sandringham 7 (JM719/G-AKCO/VH-APG/F-OBIP) – Museé De L'air, Le Bourget, Paris

JM719's early history would have followed a similar path to that of JM715. Starting life as a Mk III, JM719 was also delivered to the Air Ministry, but was destined never to enter service with an operational squadron. In April 1945, JM719 was also brought out of storage and moved to the FBMU at Caird's Yard, to be converted to Mk V standard.

However, JM719 did see service with 302 FTU, which operated from Lough Erne, training crews to ferry flying boats to overseas units. It is quite possible that JM719, one of 77 Mk Vs to serve with 302 FTU, remained with this unit until it was disbanded on 1 April 1946.

Placed in storage with 57 MU, the Sunderland was sold back to Short Brothers in May 1947 and converted to a Sandringham 7. Before the year was over it had been registered as G-AKCO and entered service with BOAC under the name *St George*. The aircraft was employed on Far East routes during its uneventful BOAC service, which came to an abrupt end in 1950.

In 1954, the Sandringham enjoyed a second wind when it was purchased by Capt Sir George Taylor, taken to Australia and reregistered as VH-APG. The flying boat was also renamed *Frigate Bird III* and was used for charter cruises around New Guinea and the many islands to the east.

In 1958, the flying boat was sold again, this time to the French Company Reseau Aerien Interinsulaire (RAI) and re-registered again as F-OBIP. The aircraft was mainly employed flying regular tourist services between Tahiti and the Society and Tuamotu Islands. Painted in a bright green and white livery, the Sandringham continued this service on a weekly basis until 1966 but was not fully retired from the air until 1970.

It then languished until 1978, when the Musee de L'Air at Le Bourget showed an interest in preserving the flying boat. Not long after, the Sandringham was dismantled and shipped to France by the French Navy to Le Bourget.

Sir Gordon Taylor's Sandringham 7 G-AKCO *Frigate Bird III* at Cowes in October 1954. (*Flight* via Martyn Chorlton)

Left: Ex-RAI F-OBIP languishing in Tahiti during the early 1970s, with an uncertain future ahead of it. (Via Martyn Chorlton)

Below: F-OBIP at Le Bourget in 1979, having arrived courtesy of the French Navy the previous year. (Alain Picollet)

Short Sunderland Mk III/Mk V (ML796) – Imperial War Museum (IWM), Duxford, Cambridge

Originally one of a batch of 75 Sunderland Mk IIIs ordered from Short Brothers, ML796 was instead destined to become the first production Mk V. ML796 was delivered to Calshot on 15 May 1945, joining 228 Squadron at Pembroke Dock not long afterwards.

An uneventful tour of duty was followed by a spell with 4 OTU that began on 3 March 1946. This short tour came to an end on 10 July 1946, when the Sunderland joined hundreds of other flying boats already in storage at 57 MU.

The Berlin Airlift saw ML796 prepared for service again, this time with 230 Squadron. ML796 took part in Operation *Plainfaire*, which saw both 201 and 230 squadrons fly a shuttle service from Finkenwerder on the Elbe in Hamburg to Lake Havel in Berlin.

Surplus to RAF requirements again by late 1949, ML796 was one of a batch of Sunderlands selected for further service with the Aeronavale (French Navy air arm). Selected on 20 December 1949, by June 1950, the aircraft was being overhauled at Belfast and, on 4 August 1951, it was handed over to the French Navy. ML796 served with Flottille 7FE from Dakar for its entire French service until December 1960.

The Sunderland was then returned to France and stored at Lanveoc-Poulmic, until it was bought in 1965 by M. R. Bertin. It was used as a disco at Maisden-le-Riviere until 1969 when it was moved to La Baule and converted into a restaurant and nightclub. Unfortunately, a few years later a motorway was planned to pass straight through the site where the Sunderland was parked and, in a desperate bid to save it, Bertin offered the aircraft for free to anyone who could remove it. Luckily, the IWM took advantage of the opportunity, and, on 9 July 1975, the Sunderland arrived at Duxford in five sections.

Right: Wartime photographs of ML796 are rare and even this one is only a glimpse. The flying boat is pictured on the River Medway on 3 October 1944, in its original Mk III configuration. (Via Martyn Chorlton)

Below: ML796 at La Baule in the early 1970s when it was a popular restaurant and nightclub. (Via Simon Woods)

The fuselage of ML796 being moved into Duxford's 'Superhangar' (now called AirSpace) during the early 1980s. (*Aeroplane*)

Displayed on a single supporting cradle, ML796 is a pristine example of a Sunderland Mk V. (Via Martyn Chorlton)

Short Sunderland Mk III/Mk V (ML814/NZ4108/VH-BRF/N158J/G-BJHS) – Fantasy of Flight Museum, Polk City, Florida

See Chapter 13

Short Sunderland Mk III/Mk V – RAF Museum, Hendon, London

Built by Short Brothers & Harland at Belfast, a batch of 25 Mk IIIs was delivered to the RAF between February and September 1944. Sunderland Mk III ML824 was taken on RAF charge on 30 June 1944 but was back at Belfast on 6 July to be converted to a Mk V.

On 6 November, ML824 was flown to 57 MU, where it was placed in temporary storage before heading south for Calshot on 9 February 1945. Two days later, the Sunderland joined 201 Squadron at Castle Archdale, the first Mk V to be received by the unit.

ML824 carried out 11 wartime operations with 201 Squadron, comprising ten U-Boat missions and a single convoy patrol. The most eventful of these patrols was on 2 April, when two depth charges were dropped on a fresh oil slick, believed to be a U-boat, without any visible results. ML824's 127hrs and 20mins of operational flying with 201 Squadron came to an end on 17 April, when it was transferred to 330 (Norwegian) Squadron at Sullom Voe.

Training flights and four more U-boat patrols carried ML824 to the end of World War Two. 330 Squadron then began the move to its new Norwegian base at Sola, Stavanger from 10–14 June, where the unit operated under 129 Wing, RAF, in the transport role. Flying took place six days a week from Stavanger to Bergen and Trondheim, sometimes continuing on to Skattora, a seaplane base near Tromsø. It was while approaching Skattora on 1 July 1945 that ML824 suffered an in-flight fire in the port outer engine and the flying boat had to be left behind. The damaged engine was later removed; a fairing was made to replace it and, on 1 September, the Sunderland was flown on three engines from Tromsø to Calshot. By 19 September, the aircraft was in store at Alness and SOC.

ML824 became the last flying boat to leave Alness on 19 May 1948, when the station was closed down. The following day, the Sunderland was under the charge of 57 MU and was one of several set aside for possible service during the Berlin Airlift but was not used.

On 25 August 1950, ML824 was back at Belfast for a full overhaul, with little more than 306.10 flying hours on the airframe. By October, the work was completed and, on 26 October, ML824 was flown to Pembroke Dock to become one of 14 Sunderlands selected to operate with the Aeronavale.

ML824 went on to serve with Flotille F7, 27F and 50s and, apart from a return to Short & Harland at Belfast for an overhaul, the aircraft served continuously with the Aeronavale until 1961. By this time, the opportunity had been missed to preserve an RAF Sunderland that had served, although ML797 of 205/209 Squadron based at Seletar was planned for preservation. Sadly, the flying boat was written off when the Sunderland slipped off a beaching gear turntable.

When news of this came through, poultry farmer and aviation enthusiast Peter M. Thomas began an appeal to raise £15,000 to purchase a Sunderland from the RNZAF and have it flown back to the UK. Technical and financial problems scuppered the idea, but the Aeronavale was still flying three Sunderlands, prompting Mr Thomas to write a letter to the French. In the meantime, the Short Sunderland Trust was formed, and the French responded by offering ML824 to the Trust free of charge.

It was 24 March 1961 when ML824, wearing the French code 50.S.9, began its final flight from Lanveoc-Pouloc near Brest, bound for Pembroke Dock. En route, the Sunderland rendezvoused with a pair of 201 Squadron Shackletons from St Mawgan, which escorted ML824 from the Scilly Islands via St. Davids and on to Pembroke Dock. In front of huge crowds, the three aircraft circled the dock before the Sunderland landed at 1136hrs, ending a flying career that covered 2,700 flying hours. The following day, ML824 was removed from the water for the last time for a lengthy handover ceremony; the Sunderland was later moved to a leased site in a corner of the dockyard. From June 1961, the aircraft was open to the public and was cared for by the secretary of the Sunderland Trust, Sqn Ldr F. E. Godfrey. Incredibly, the flying boat was visited by over 10,000 people during its first season on display. This number peaked in 1967 with 20,000 visitors, but the following year, Sqn Ldr Godfrey contacted the RAF Museum to suggest that it should approach the aircraft's trustees about buying ML824.

Sadly, Sqn Ldr Godfrey passed away in December 1969. However, he had already secured the future of the aircraft, and, on 11 January 1971, all Trust assets were transferred to the Trustees of the RAF Museum. Just prior to the lease expiring on the land on which it was located, the Sunderland was moved to an empty hangar at Pembroke Dock in March, where a party from 71 MU set about dismantling the flying boat. All components of the Sunderland were sent by road direct to Hendon – with the exception of the fuselage, which sailed to London on 10 March in a Royal Corps of Transport landing craft. On 16 March, the landing craft docked in Dagenham and from there the fuselage was transported on its side to Hendon, demolishing at least one set of traffic lights en route!

Although some re-erection work took place not long after ML824 arrived, the Sunderland remained under a collection of old parachutes in the Graham-White hangar until engineers from St Athan and Abingdon began reassembling the aircraft in September 1976. By October, the Sunderland was moved to a position outside the museum by a team of Royal Engineers from 39 Engineer Regiment, from Waterbeach north of Cambridge.

In 1978, the Sunderland reached its final resting place in Hendon's RAF Museum and since then, continued restoration work has kept ML824 in the excellent condition we see it in today.

ML824 on its way back to England from France on 24 March 1961, being escorted by a pair of 201 Squadron Shackletons. (Via Martyn Chorlton)

Aeronavale Sunderland Mk V ML824/50.S.9 pictured over St Davids on 24 March 1961 on its final flight into Pembroke Dock. (*Aeroplane*)

Another view of ML824 wearing its French Aeronavale code 50.S.9, but always, as with all French Sunderlands, retaining its original RAF serial. (Via Martyn Chorlton)

Right and below: ML824 on its way from Dagenham docks on 16 March 1971, to its final and current resting place at Hendon. (*Aeroplane*)

ML824 was moved to its location in Hendon's Battle of Britain Museum in 1978. (Via Martyn Chorlton)

Short Sunderland Mk V (SZ584/G-AHJR/NZ4115) – Museum of Transportation and Technology (MOTAT) Aviation Unit, Auckland

The first on our preservation list to have actually been built as a Mk V was SZ584, one of 28 (from an order of 40) built by Short Brothers & Harland at Belfast.

After being taken on RAF charge, SZ584 was loaned to BOAC for evaluation and given the civilian registration G-AHJR on 2 May 1946. The Sunderland was returned to the RAF on 16 April 1948 but was placed in storage, most likely at 57 MU. On 2 April 1952, SZ584 was transferred to the FBSU at Wig Bay where it was refurbished in preparation for service with the RNZAF.

On 4 September 1953, SZ584 was transferred to the RNZAF and re-registered as NZ4115. The aircraft was prepared for service with the RNZAF at 1 Aircraft Depot, Hobsonville, before being allocated to 5 Squadron RNZAF. During its service, NZ4115 was give the codes 'A', 'B' and finally 'Q' before the Sunderland was SOC on 9 December 1966. On 22 December, the Sunderland was 'gifted' to MOTAT in airworthy condition at Hobsonville, where it remained until 25 February 1967. It was then towed to Meola Creek and winched overland to MOTAT, where it remains today in its final RNZAF markings.

NZ4115 at Auckland's Museum of Transportation and Technology (MOTAT) not long after its arrival from Hobsonville in 1967.

Short Seaford Mk I/Solent 3 (NJ203/G-AKNP/VH-TOB/N9946F) – Oakland Aviation Museum, Oakland, California

NJ203 began its life as part of a small batch of Short Seafords that were a development of the Sunderland, originally designated the Mk IV. Virtually all the RAF's planned Seafords were converted to Solent 3s, including the fourth production aircraft, NJ203, which was delivered on 24 October 1946.

After briefly operating with 201 Squadron for trials work, the Solent was re-registered as G-AKNP and entered service with BOAC under the name *City of Cardiff* on 31 July 1949. BOAC service was destined to be short, however, and on 2 November 1950, the Solent flew its last service from Augusta to Southampton. After being placed in open storage, the Solent was sold to P. G. Taylor's Trans Oceanic Airways (TOA) on 23 March 1951 and delivered to Sydney on 4 April. Now registered as VH-TOB and named *Star of Papua* (although photographic evidence shows that the name *City of Cardiff* was retained for quite some time), the Solent operated on various routes, including services to Grafton, Hobart, Port Moresby and the Solomon Islands–New Caledonia route.

TOA then passed into liquidation and VH-TOB flew its last revenue service for the company on 15–16 April 1953. Cancelled from the Australian Aircraft Register on 12 February 1954, the Solent was registered in the USA as N9946F on 1 May 1954. Eleven days later, with Capt B. Monkton at the controls, the Solent left Sydney bound for Honolulu via Fiji and Canton Island.

The Solent was now operated by South Pacific Airlines (SPAL) and once it had been renamed *Isle of Tahiti*, the aircraft was operated on the Honolulu via Christmas Island and back to Tahiti service. Refurbished by Transocean Air Lines at Oakland, California, the flying boat continued a similar service from December 1958, which also took in Papeete. Unfortunately, a decision by the British government to use Christmas Island for nuclear testing put paid to the Solent's route and, by 1959, the flying boat was returned to Oakland. Sold to the Hughes Tool Company, *Isle of Tahiti* remained in open storage throughout the 1960s.

In February 1973, N9946F was sold to H&M Airline Services, and then to R&H Gottelli the following month. By now, the condition of the aircraft was deteriorating and, under the threat of being scrapped, the Solent was bought by Rick and Randy Grant for restoration to flying condition and, in 1978, they renamed it *Halcyon*. The restoration group itself was originally named the Friends of Halcyon but was later renamed Seaflite instead.

Today, the Solent has beaten the odds and is on public display at the Oakland Aviation Museum at Oakland, California. Thoughtfully restored, the Solent is resplendent in an all-white scheme as BOAC's *City of Cardiff* G-AKNP, the only complete Mk III survivor.

Solent 3 N9946F at rest in Tahiti whilst serving with South Pacific Air Lines (SPAL).

Short Solent 3 G-AKNP *City of Cardiff* was converted from Seaford NJ203. (Allan King)

Short Solent 4 (ZK-AMO) – MOTAT Aviation Unit, Auckland

Prior to TEAL's Sandringhams being grounded because of engine overheating problems, the airline had already placed an order for the more capable Solent Mk IVs as replacements. Four aircraft were ordered from Short Brothers, including c/n SH-1559 ZK-AMO, which TEAL named *Aranui*.

Delivered in November 1949, TEAL's Solents immediately brought the trans-Tasman flight time down to 6½ hours. Up to 1950, TEAL only operated the Mechanics Bay, Auckland, to Rose Bay, Sydney, route but the arrival of the Solent gave the company the opportunity to expand and, on 6 June 1950, a second route from Auckland to Fiji (Suva) began.

From December 1951, ZK-AMO was employed on the Auckland–Tahiti service – also known as the 'Coral Route'. More like an airborne cruise than a scheduled flight, the Coral Route took in Samoa, the Cook Islands and Tonga.

On 14 September 1960, ZK-AMO flew its last flight for TEAL from Fiji to Tahiti, bringing an end to the big flying boat services, which had been superseded by more efficient land-based airliners.

Luckily, the importance and rarity of the Solent 4 was recognised very early on and ZK-AMO survives today as the only complete example of its mark in the world.

Fully restored to its former glory inside and out, Solent 4 is safely under cover at MOTAT in its original TEAL colours.

Chapter 13

The Last One Flying

O n a dull July day in 1993, a flying boat took off from Southampton Water and set course for Ireland and the North Atlantic. It was the very last airworthy Short Sunderland in the world, and it was leaving the UK for a new home in Florida. Although valiant efforts were made to find a base to keep the aircraft in Britain, the sheer costs involved in maintaining a seaplane defeated those who had battled for 14 years to keep a flying Sunderland in the UK. What made it difficult was the fact that the Sunderland was a flying boat – a seaplane – it could not alight on tarmac or grass. A large four-engined wheeled aircraft, such as a B-17 or Lancaster, can be accommodated with reasonable ease at an airfield and even be found space in a hangar, but a flying boat needs a large stretch of water from which to operate. It also needs a substantial slipway to get it out of the water and onto dry land. Sadly, places that could house such an aircraft are few and far between on the British Isles and some owner-operators of suitable locations did not want the aircraft. Suffice to say, the aircraft went abroad.

ML814/G-BJHS, the world's last flying Sunderland flying boat, is captured over the south of England in early 1993, before Kermit Weeks took the aircraft across the Atlantic. (*Aeroplane*)

Built in Northern Ireland

Sir Arthur Gouge had designed a remarkable series of flying boats, the most successful of which was the Sunderland. In March 1944, the 63rd example to be built at Short & Harland's Queen's Island, Belfast factory – one of a batch of Sunderlands destined for the RAF – was ML814. There are no records of how ML814 spent these early days; we know that its systems would have been checked at Queen's Island before being towed down the slipway into Belfast Lough and moored along with other examples of the type awaiting test flying. These flights were only of short duration to check that the aircraft handled well in the air before being handed over to the RAF. On 25 March 1944, ML814 was flown from Belfast to Wig Bay near Stranraer where 57 MU fitted out the aircraft with the necessary service equipment, including the ASV Mk 3 radar, prior to it being allocated to a Coastal Command squadron.

On 24 April 1944, Flt Lt Aubrey Poole and a crew of four arrived at Wig Bay to test fly ML814 before ferrying it to Pembroke Dock and life with 201 Squadron. Poole started up the engines and, at 1505hrs, took off from Wig Bay. ML814 held no surprises and, just 90 minutes later, alighted on the waters around Pembroke Dock. The following day, Poole and his crew flew the aircraft down to Calshot for various modifications. The defensive armament was probably installed at this stage and the squadron identification letters – NS-R – were applied before ML814 was flown to Mount Batten near Plymouth.

At this point, ML814 was allocated to Fg Off David A. Easton and his crew; on 9 May, they took the Sunderland on a test flight to familiarise themselves with the area. Easton visited ML814 in 1992 and was able to clearly recall that first flight and others he had made at the controls of the Sunderland. He described the brand new ML814 as feeling 'tight and fresh, like a new car'.

In Service

Easton took ML814 back to Pembroke Dock and, on 11 May 1944, carried out a night flare dropping exercise and radar training over Carmarthen Bay. It was all part of the preparation for Operation *Overlord* – the Allied invasion of Europe. Easton recalled seeing the hundreds of ships moored in Southampton Water and the Solent, as well as the massive Mulberry Harbour caissons, although at the time he did not know what they were for. On 14 May, ML814 – under Easton's command – slipped moorings at 1305hrs and taxied out on its first operational patrol. Fully armed with bombs, fuel, ammunition, flares and stores, the aircraft took off and headed for the North Atlantic. These patrols were routine and rarely was the enemy sighted. Ask any former Coastal Command crew member and he will tell you about the boring and cold hours spent over the grey Atlantic. Nevertheless, it was an important defence role and had to be carried out. After over 13 hours on patrol, ML814 returned to its moorings at 0230hrs the next day. 'Nothing happened', recalled Easton in 1992, 'and we saw nothing but then that was normal!'

While the Sunderland was armed with three gun turrets, they only held the standard RAF 0.303in Colt-Browning machine guns. These may have been the last word in 1939, but by 1944, they were seriously out-gunned by the cannon-equipped German fighters. Consequently, Coastal Command Sunderland crews hoped they would not meet a Junkers Ju 88 during their patrols! Although Sunderland gunners did account for many enemy aircraft, they had to get quite close for the Brownings to be effective.

ML814 had become accustomed to uneventful operations, and, on 19 May, Easton and his crew flew a standard night anti-submarine patrol. However, as they neared the patrol area, the ASV radar picked up a contact. Front gunner Sgt Nicholson was the first to spot the Ju 88 flying towards the Sunderland. Easton remembered that: 'The Ju got closer and all the gunners were hoping he would not fire before they had him in range. He flew towards us and then circled us before waggling his wings, saying "Good Morning" I suppose, and then he carried on flying northwards. No shots were exchanged! We thought he may have been an unarmed meteorological aircraft on his way to his designated area.'

Further routine patrols followed as D-day approached and took place, with ML814 involved in looking for U-boats in the Bay of Biscay; it did not sight any submarines. Easton and his crew were rested while another crew took over their aircraft for a series of patrols, one of them a night sortie in low cloud, very heavy rain and fog. Peter Lillingston, who was second pilot to Fg Off R. A. N. McCready, recalled that they landed in the Scilly Isles before returning to Pembroke Dock at about 0730hrs. Easton and his crew were back on patrol with ML814 in August but had nothing to report. It appeared that the Germans had gone into hiding, which is, in effect, what they had achieved, with the fitting of snorkels to enable the diesel engines to 'breathe' while at periscope depth. This meant that spotting such a small object in the water was almost impossible. Easton and his crew completed their operational tour of duty on 1 September 1944, with a final patrol south of Fastnet. However, ML814 stayed on with 201 Squadron and was flown by different crews on patrols until 4 October, when it was moved to Calshot for a complete overhaul.

Meanwhile, 201 Squadron moved to Castle Archdale, and ML814 was allocated to 422 Squadron in December and was back at Pembroke Dock with the new squadron letters DG-N. Even though, by now, the Germans had no bases in France, the anti-submarine patrols continued. ML814 took part in several patrols, generally with a crew under the command of Flt Lt L. E. Giles, but other 422 Squadron captains and their crews also flew the aircraft. Christmas 1944 came and went and ML814 carried on with routine patrols and various exercises. Then, on 19 February 1945, ML814 was off the squadron's books and en route back to Queen's Island for a refit.

Here, Sunderlands were being upgraded. The sometimes-unreliable Bristol Pegasus units that had been fitted from build were replaced with the more powerful Pratt & Whitney Twin Wasp engines. The makers removed the dorsal turret, and two 0.50 calibre waist guns were installed in new hatches aft of the trailing edge of the wing. When ML814 emerged in late April 1945, it was as a Mk V and was allocated to 330 Squadron based at Sullom Voe. A new set of squadron letters, WH-A, appeared on the side of ML814 and it made its first operational flight on 2 May. Capt George Evensen was in the left-hand seat piloting ML814 on an anti-submarine sweep as one of the escort aircraft for a Russia-bound convoy. They did not sight anything sinister, just local fishing boats that they flew low over as part of the sweep. The war was coming to an end and ML814 flew one more sortie on 7 May, the day before the formal surrender of Germany, and reported that nothing had been sighted on patrol. Although the war had ended and signals had been sent to all U-boat captains to return, it was possible that some had not received the signal or had decided to make a run for a neutral country. As it was, several U-boat captains scuttled their boats rather than surrender them. Consequently, Coastal Command continued their patrols for some time.

This is the only known photograph of ML814 in its service career and shows the aircraft during its time with 303 (Norwegian) Squadron about to alight at Sullom Voe. (Royal Norwegian Air Force)

Above: Newly registered as N158C and named *Southern Cross*, the Sandringham 4 serves with Antilles Air Boats, Virgin Islands. In the foreground is N158J *Excalibur VIII*, ex-ML814, now in the hands of Kermit Weeks. (Via Martyn Chorlton)

Left: VH-BRF off-loading passengers at Rose Bay, Sydney, whilst serving with Ansett Flying boat Services during the early 1970s.

G-BJHS moored near Tower Bridge in August 1982. (C. N. Wilson)

Above: G-BJHS displays Imperial Airways insignia in commemoration of the pre-war airline. The flying boat was visited by several ex-Imperial Airways staff during its brief time on the River Thames in August 1982. (Via Martyn Chorlton)

Below left: The flight deck has been altered over the years, and many new or different instruments were added by the RNZAF and Ansett. (Via François Prins)

Below right: Looking aft towards the area where the rear gun turret would have been fitted. During military service, there would have been a work bench fitted to the right. Note the control lines at the top of the picture for tailplane and rudder. (Via François Prins)

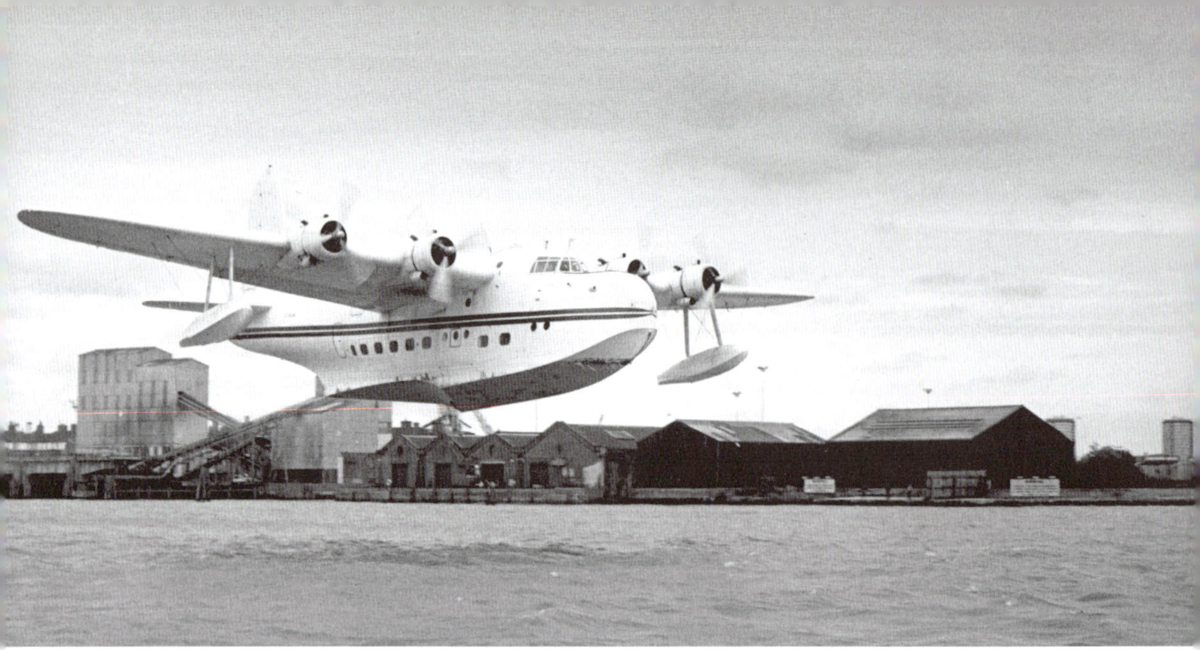

Above: **September 1982 saw G-BJHS (ML814) leave London for a new home at Calshot near Southampton. At Calshot, the Sunderland was taken out of the water and beached near the old slipway where Schneider Trophy aircraft once entered the water. (Via François Prins)**

Left: **A move from Calshot took ML814 to the old Royal Navy dockyard at Chatham not far from Rochester, where most of the Empire flying boats were built and launched. (Via François Prins)**

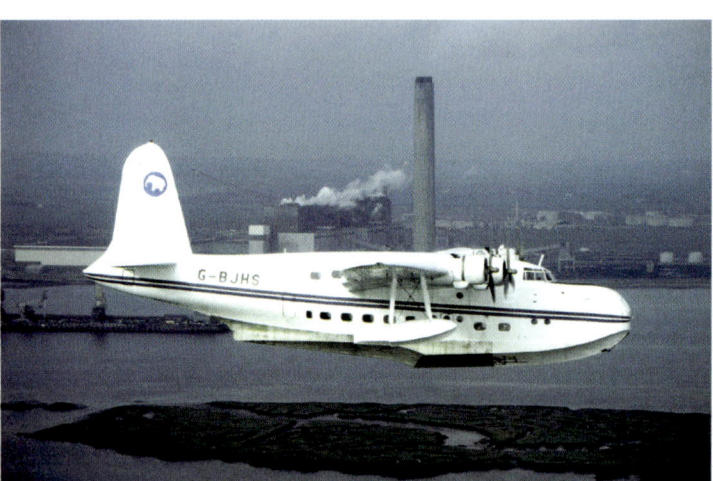

Foreign Service

On 11 May, ML814 – under the command of Capt Evensen – was chosen to escort a convoy of warships carrying Crown Prince Olav of Norway and ministers of the Norwegian government to Oslo. Joining ML814 were several Mosquitoes and Beaufighters. 330 Squadron was relocated to Sola in Norway and, on 14 June, ML814 left Scotland for Norway and peacetime flying duties. These included a shuttle service between various locations in Norway: from the safety of Bergen and Trondheim to the difficult waters of Tromsø. It is worth noting that although ML814 and other 330 Squadron Sunderlands were operating a military passenger service – sometimes with over 25 people on board – the aircraft remained standard with no added benefits of extra heating or comfortable seats. 330 Squadron reverted from the RAF to the Royal Norwegian Air Force in December 1945. The Sunderlands were then returned and ferried back from Sola to the UK by RAF crews.

All the aircraft ended up at Killadeas on Lough Erne, where many were scrapped. However, ML814 was flown to Wig Bay and placed in the care of 57 MU; it inhibited the engines, stripped out guns and radios and other removable items and covered windows and gun turrets, before mothballing the aircraft for storage. In 1952, New Zealand placed an order with Short Brothers for 16 refurbished

To ferry the Sunderland from Calshot to Chatham, the owners enlisted the help of Canadian Martin Mars pilot Reg Young. This shows him about to alight on the river near Chatham. (Via François Prins)

Sunderlands; ML814 was among those selected. Along with the other 15 aircraft, ML814 was made airworthy and flown to Queen's Island in May 1952.

The aircraft were virtually rebuilt and updated with the latest radio and radar fittings. They were also renumbered for the RNZAF – ML814 became NZ4108. On 21 May 1953, ML814 was flown to Wig Bay for testing, and on 28 May was handed over to an RNZAF crew for a flight to Calshot. The following day, ML814 left under the command of Flt Lt Edward 'Ted' Tomkins, on the first leg of a 16-day journey to Lauthala Bay, Suva, Fiji, where 5 RNZAF Squadron was based. This aircraft was the first of two to arrive, NZ4105 being the other, and was immediately pressed into use around the Pacific islands. Medical evacuation flights were a regular part of the squadron's duties in an area where medical care was not easily obtained.

After more than four years in Fiji, NZ4108 was transferred to 6 Squadron and left the Pacific on 5 January 1956, with new code letters XX-D replacing KN-B. Based at Hobsonville, Auckland, the squadron flew training missions, as well as search and rescue flights, but, on 21 June 1957, XX-D was placed in long-term storage at the base.

Civilian Duty

From 1947, flying boats had been used to fly between Sydney and Lord Howe Island and when, in 1963, Sandringham *Pacific Chieftain* was wrecked in a storm, a search was made for a replacement. This was found among the stored RNZAF Sunderlands, and NZ4108 was chosen for conversion to a passenger aircraft. It is worth noting that NZ4108/ML814 is often erroneously referred to as a Sandringham but it remains a Sunderland, as the conversion work is quite different and was not carried out by Short Brothers. On 18 December 1963, an Ansett crew arrived and ferried the aircraft to Rose Bay in Sydney. Here the turrets were removed and faired over. Much of the interior, along with radios and heaters, came from the salvaged *Pacific Chieftain*, which helped to speed up the work. Registered as VH-BRF *Islander*, the aircraft was ready for duty on 3 October 1964.

Eight months after it had commenced passenger duties, *Islander* was washed ashore on Lord Howe Island during a fierce storm. Fortunately, the hull was not damaged, although a float was broken. The Ansett maintenance team were able to re-float the Sunderland and fly it back to Sydney on 10 June – ten days after it had been blown ashore. As traffic to Lord Howe increased, it was decided to build a metalled runway on the island, and this commenced in March 1974; eventually, the flying boat service came to an end.

New ownership

Charles Blair, an American record-breaking pilot, USAF brigadier general and senior Pan Am captain, visited Sydney on a regular basis and on one occasion he flew on board one of the Ansett flying boats. When they came up for sale in 1974, he bought them for his Antilles Air Boats operation based in the US Virgin Islands. Registered N158J and christened *Excalibur VIII* – he named his various aircraft *Excalibur* – the Sunderland flew out of Rose Bay on 25 September 1974, with Lloyd Maundrell as captain and Blair being checked out on type. The aircraft crossed the Pacific via several islands, including a stop at Pearl Harbor before landing at Long Beach, where N158J was moored astern of RMS *Queen Mary*.

On 6 October, the Sunderland took off for the flight across the US with Capts Blair and Ron Gillies. They flew to Eagle Mountain Lake, north of Dallas, and then on to Washington, where the aircraft landed on the Potomac. Next came New York, landing near the Statue of Liberty and then on to Boston for refuelling and the final journey of the 9,900-mile (15,900km) ferry flight to St Croix in the US Virgin Islands. On 9 December, the second aircraft, Sandringham VH-BRC, arrived at St Croix.

Unfortunately, the US Federal Aviation Authority (FAA) would not certify the aircraft for passenger operations as there had never been a Sandringham on the US civil register. Consequently, it was decided to place the aircraft on the British Colonial register, but *Excalibur VIII* was immediately excluded as Short had not carried out the conversion. The Sandringham was registered as VP-LVE and, reluctantly, granted certification. The UK CAA's refusal to budge on the Sunderland meant that it was placed in storage at Isla Grande Airport in Puerto Rico, where it deteriorated.

In 1978, Edward Hulton heard about the two Short flying boats and wrote to Charles Blair to ask if he would be interested in selling one of them. Blair wrote back that he would consider the matter. Hulton telephoned St Croix on 2 September, only to be told that Blair had been killed in an accident an hour earlier. Apparently, he was flying passengers from St Croix to St Thomas and an engine on the Grumman Goose failed; he tried to complete the flight, but the port float struck the water and the aircraft cartwheeled and broke up. Blair and three passengers were killed. Hulton let the matter rest for the time being.

Blair's widow, actress Maureen O'Hara, had sold Antilles Air Boats to the Resorts International chain, and Ron Gillies had been tasked with disposing of the two stored Short flying boats. Hulton went to see the aircraft in May 1979 and soon concluded a deal to purchase *Excalibur VIII*. Work to get the aircraft ready commenced, but it later transpired that the US firm that carried out the work had done so in a slip-shod manner, and most of it had to be redone when the aircraft was in Europe.

November 1980 saw the aircraft towed out of the hangar, and the engines – which had been totally rebuilt by Scottish Aviation – were tested. All appeared well and the aircraft was flight tested, but – even though it was on the American register – the FAA would not allow it to operate in US-controlled air space; they only would allow it to fly through if it was en route to a foreign destination. For the next few months, the Sunderland flew between the islands of the Caribbean, but the shoddy work began to manifest, and the hull showed signs of corrosion. The decision was made to fly the aircraft to Europe, with Capts Brian Monkton and Keith Sissons on the flight deck. On 27 March 1981, the aircraft left St Croix for Bermuda and the Atlantic crossing to France. Originally, it had been intended to cross to the Azores and Lisbon, but weather conditions dictated a route up the eastern seaboard of the US to Canada and then on to Ireland and the UK. Problems with the radios kept the Sunderland in Bermuda until

16 May, when it took off for Gander. The next day, the aircraft set off to cross the Atlantic and, on 18 May, landed at Lough Derg, County Donegal, after 13hrs and 35mins in the air. A few days later, *Excalibur VIII* landed on the Solent at Calshot and stayed moored for several days before crossing to Marignane in the South of France, where there was a slipway and a hangar for work to begin on correcting the shoddy US restoration. Aérospatiale was contracted to carry out the task. It was at this stage that Peter Smith joined the aircraft and became the one man who held the story together over the next ten years.

Right: The Royal Electrical and Mechanical Engineers (REME) from Marchwood were recruited to help move G-BJHS up the slipway at Calshot on 14 December 1982. (Via Martyn Chorlton)

Below: Moored near Rochester Castle after having just flown back from Ireland, G-BJHS still carries the Ryanair titles, which were quickly painted out. (Via François Prins)

Back in Britain

Smith was not an aircraft engineer when he started but, by the time ML814 was sold, he had sat and passed the various engineering tests. Edward Hulton was keen to bring ML814 – now on the UK register as G-BJHS with Guernsey-based Sunderland Ltd – to London as soon as work was completed. On 6 August 1982, the aircraft left France and landed on the River Thames to taxi up to a mooring aft of HMS *Belfast* and opposite the Tower of London. A Nimrod MR.2 from 201 Squadron joined G-BJHS for the flight over London.

The Sunderland was visited by several former Imperial Airways flying boat crews and ex-Coastal Command veterans, some of whom had flown ML814 during its service career. The time came to leave London and, on 19 October, the aircraft took off and headed for Calshot, where it was moored until 14 December when the Royal Electrical and Mechanical Engineers (REME) from Marchwood helped to get it up the slipway to the hard standing at the top.

Sunderland Ltd had hoped that a permanent home could be found for G-BJHS and that it would be given an AOC to fly passengers, but the CAA refused to consider the application as the aircraft had been converted by someone other than the original manufacturer and that did not meet its strict rules. No matter how hard the case was argued, it would not budge even though it liked the aircraft. Eventually, Hampshire County Council and Calshot, which charged a considerable fee for the hard standing, wanted the aircraft off their land. Help was at hand, however, in the form of Malcolm Moulton of GEC-Avionics and the Medway branch of the Royal Aeronautical Society. He had found space, under cover, at Chatham Historic Dockyard and, on 20 November 1984, G-BJHS left Calshot for the Medway. This could have been the saving of the aircraft for the nation, but due to various factions, none of the proposals from Medway and others came to anything. To add to the woes, on 16 October 1987 – 50 years to the day when the prototype Sunderland had flown – the last flying example was badly damaged in the fierce storms that hit the British Isles.

Peter Smith had valiantly tried to hold the 20-ton aircraft, but it was bounced like a toy, fell off the tail trolley, damaging the stern post, and rocked on the main beaching gear to such an extent that the starboard wing hit the ground at force and was bent upwards. G-BJHS was offered for sale as it was and discussions were held with interested parties in the UK and Australia, but these came to nothing and Sunderland Ltd decided to rebuild the aircraft. Ryanair – before it became a budget operation – showed interest in operating G-BJHS from Foynes, where a new museum had been opened, and when work was complete, the Sunderland departed for Ireland carrying the Ryanair titles. However, this was short-lived, and the aircraft was back in the Solent soon afterwards. Little happened with G-BJHS for the next few weeks, although it was flown at the Great Warbirds Gathering at West Malling in 1989 and carried out some film work, one with Pan Am titles applied to the nose.

On 16 June 1990, operating once more from Calshot, G-BJHS carried out four air displays: Biggin Hill, Coningsby, Fleetlands and Hamble, the last two side-by-side. Then, on 28 June, the Sunderland left for Lake Windermere, where 35 Sunderlands were built during the war, to join in the annual festival. Back at Calshot, the aircraft was brought up the slipway once more; it was offered for sale via auction but was not sold. However, there was renewed interest from Norway and Australia. Both countries were keen to purchase the flying boat and discussions continued. The Norwegians dropped out, leaving the Australians in the frame. They were having difficulty in assembling the required funds and Sunderland Ltd was keen to sell the aircraft as money to maintain it was now exhausted.

Kermit Weeks, the well known American collector and operator of historic aircraft, was attracted by the fact that G-BJHS was the only airworthy Sunderland and made an offer. This was accepted and plans to ferry the aircraft across the Atlantic commenced. Ken Emmott, who had flown G-BJHS for some time, instructed Weeks in the art of flying the Sunderland and signed him off before the time

Above: Chatham, only weeks before the flying boat was damaged in a fierce storm on 16 October 1987.

Right: A fine study of G-BJHS during a rare air-to-air photograph before the flying boat departed for the US. (*Aeroplane*)

came to fly across the Atlantic. On 20 July 1993, the aircraft left Calshot and crossed the Atlantic via Ireland and Iceland; it put in at the latter to have the radios repaired. These had failed soon after G-BJHS left Ireland and messages could only be transmitted on the UHF band via a host aircraft. G-BJHS was escorted for part of the way by a Nimrod from 201 Squadron, which passed messages as required. G-BJHS used the callsign 'Sunderland Flying Boat' and this was picked up by scheduled airliners crossing at far higher altitudes and when Ken Emmot made the call: 'Sunderland Flying boat', he was heard and, rather amusingly, answered by the captain of an American airliner with the words: 'Gee you guys still on patrol? Pass your message'.

The Sunderland landed on Lake Ontario before flying down to Oshkosh for the EAA event; it stayed a year and, in 1994, landed on the lake excavated by Weeks at Polk City, Florida. The engines were shut down and the aircraft was moved into the hangar at the Museum of Flight. There it has stayed silent and static ever since. Occasionally it is brought out into the sunshine and at Christmas it is, or has been in the past, decked out with coloured lights. Despite these jaunty efforts, it is a great pity that the last airworthy Sunderland has ended up beached so far from home.

Sunderland V G-BJHS being escorted by Canadian Vickers-built OA-10A-VI Canso in the colours of 210 Squadron, in which Flt Lt J. Cruickshank won his VC.

Chapter 14

War Boats and Civvie Boats

THE PROTOTYPE – SHORT S.25 SUNDERLAND

FIRST FLOWN: 16 October 1937

POWERPLANT:(first) four 950hp Bristol Pegasus Xs; (second) four 1,050hp Bristol Pegasus XIIIs

DIMENSIONS: Span: 112ft 9in; Length: 85ft 8in; Height (fin-top): 32ft 10½in; Wing area: 1,487sq ft

WEIGHT: Empty: 28,290lb; Max take-off: 45,700lb

PERFORMANCE: Max speed: 210mph; Initial climb: 1,200ft/min; Ceiling: 20,500ft; Still air range: 2,880 miles; Loaded range 2,530 miles

ARMAMENT: Nil

Sunderland prototype K4774 at Felixstowe with the MAEE in 1938. The flying boat was destined to spend most of its time with the MAEE. (*Aeroplane*)

SUNDERLAND MK I

FIRST FLOWN: 21 April 1938

POWERPLANT: Four 1,100hp Bristol Pegasus XXIIs

DIMENSIONS: Span: 112ft 9in; Length: 85ft 8in; Height (fin-top): 32ft 10½in; Wing area: 1,487sq ft

WEIGHT: Empty: 28,290lb; Max take-off: 45,700lb

PERFORMANCE: Max speed: 210mph; Initial climb: 1,200ft/min; Ceiling: 20,500ft; Still air range: 2,880 miles; Loaded range 2,530 miles

ARMAMENT: Nose Turret: FN11 (1 x .303in); Tail Turret: FN13 (4 x .303in); Dorsal Hatches: 2 x .303in 'K' VGO (Vickers Gas Operated); Bomb load: 2,000lb

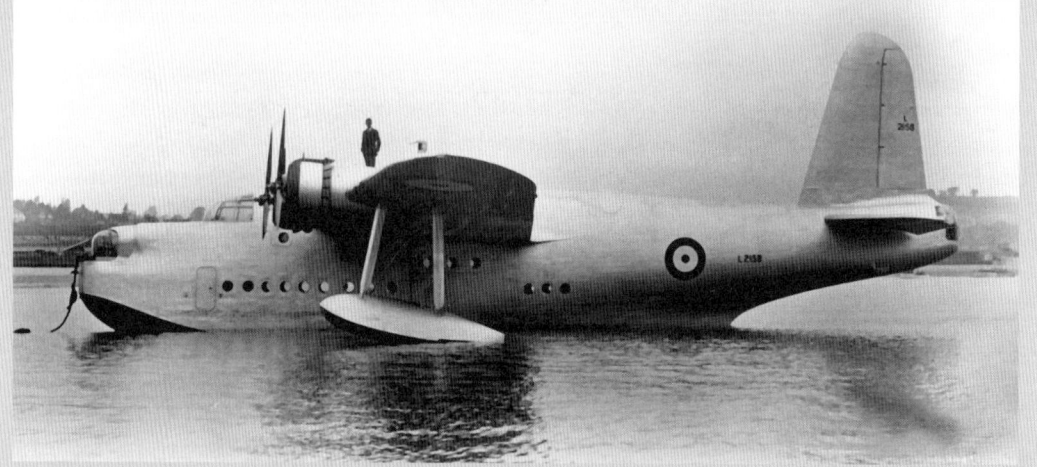

The first production Sunderland Mk I L2158 on the River Medway in April 1938. (*Aeroplane* via Martyn Chorlton)

SUNDERLAND MK II

FIRST FLOWN: August 1941

POWERPLANT: Four 965hp Bristol Pegasus XVIIIs

DIMENSIONS: Span: 112ft 9in; Length: 85ft 8in; Height (fin-top): 31ft 10½in; Wing area: 1,487sq ft

WEIGHT: Empty: 33,000lb; Max take-off: 58,000lb

PERFORMANCE: Max speed: 205mph; Initial climb: 1,200ft/min; Ceiling: 20,500ft; Still air range: 2,880 miles; Loaded range 2,530 miles

ARMAMENT: Nose Turret: FN11 (2 x .303in); Tail Turret: FN4a (4 x .303in); Dorsal Hatches: FN7 (2 x .303in); Bomb load: 2,000lb

Very rare wartime photograph of a Sunderland Mk II with the sensitive rear fuselage and underwing aerials not scrubbed out by the censor. This example is supplied by 10 Squadron RAAF. (Via Martyn Chorlton)

SUNDERLAND MK III

FIRST FLOWN: 28 June 1941

POWERPLANT: Four 965hp Bristol Pegasus XVIIIs

DIMENSIONS: Span: 112ft 9in; Length: 85ft 4in; Height (fin-top): 32ft 10½in; Wing Area: 1,487sq ft

WEIGHT: Empty: 34,500lb; Max take-off: 58,000lb

PERFORMANCE: Max speed: 210mph; Initial climb: 1,200ft/min; Ceiling: 17,200ft; Still air range: 2,880 miles; Loaded range 2,530 miles

ARMAMENT: Nose Turret: FN11 (2 x .303in). Nose fixed (some aircraft [4 x .303in]); Tail Turret: FN4a (4 x .303in); Dorsal Hatches: FN7 (2 x .303in); Bomb load: 2,000lb

The first production Sunderland Mk III has also managed to escape the censor with all aerials and sensitive equipment on display. Delivered to 10 Squadron RAAF on 29 January 1942, the flying boat was shot down by an Arado 196 over the Bay of Biscay on 21 June 1942. (Via Martyn Chorlton)

SUNDERLAND MK IV/SEAFORD MK I

FIRST FLOWN: 30 August 1944

POWERPLANT: (Mk IV) Four 1,720hp Bristol Hercules XIXs; (Seaford) Four 1,675hp Bristol Hercules 130s

DIMENSIONS: SPAN: 112ft 9½in; Length: 88ft 6¾in; Height (fin-top): 37ft 3in; Wing Area: 1,687sq ft

WEIGHT: Empty: 45,000lb; Max: 75,000lb

PERFORMANCE: Max speed: 242mph; Initial climb: 880ft/min; Ceiling: 13,000ft; Range 2,800 miles

ARMAMENT: Nose Turret: 2 x .50in; Tail Turret: 2 x .50in); Beam positions: 2 x .50in; Dorsal turret: 2 x 20mm Hispano, 2 x fixed .303in; Bomb load: 4,960lb

The Sunderland Mk IV prototype MZ269 pictured on the River Medway in April 1945. The flying boat was later converted into the prototype Seaford Mk I. (Via Martyn Chorlton)

SUNDERLAND MK V (INCLUDING GR.5 AND MR.5)

FIRST FLOWN: 1944

POWERPLANT: Four 1,200hp Pratt & Whitney 1830-90B/C/Ds

DIMENSIONS: Span: 112ft 9in; Length: 85ft 3½in; Height (fin-top): 32ft 10½in; Wing Area: 1,487sq ft

WEIGHT: Empty: 37,000lb; Max take-off: 60,000lb

PERFORMANCE: Max speed: 213mph; Initial climb: 840ft/min; Ceiling: 17,900ft; Still air range: 2,980 miles

ARMAMENT: Nose Turret: FN11 (2 x .303in); Nose fixed: 4 x .303in; Tail Turret: FN4a (4 x .303in); Dorsal Hatches: FN7 (2 x .303in), 0.5in guns on virtually post-war marks; Bomb load: 2,000lb

A Short Sunderland Mk V, unusually, at altitude in March 1945. (*Aeroplane*)

SANDRINGHAM 1, 2, 3, 4, 5, 6 AND 7

FIRST FLOWN: 1943

POWERPLANT: Four (1) Bristol Pegasus 38s; (2) Pratt & Whitney R-1830-92s; (4) Pratt & Whitney R-1830-92Cs; (5, 6, and 7) Pratt & Whitney R-1830-92Ds

DIMENSIONS: Span: 112ft 9in (all marks); Length: (1) 85ft 4¼in, (2, 3, 5, and 7) 86ft 3in; Height (fin- top): 32ft 10½in (all marks); Wing Area: 1,687sq ft (all marks)

WEIGHT: Max: (1, 2 and 3) 56,000lb, (5 and 7) 60,000lb

PERFORMANCE: Max speed: (1) 216mph, (2 and 3) 238mph, (5 and 7) 206mph; Ceiling: (1) 16,000ft, (2 and 3) 21,300ft, (5 and 7) 17,900ft; Range: (1) 2,550 miles, (2 and 3) 2,410 miles, (5 and 7) 2,440 miles

PASSENGERS: (1) Sunderland Mk III conversion for BOAC for 24 day and 16 sleeper passengers; (2) Sunderland Mk V conversion for Dodero for 45 day passengers; (3) Sunderland Mk V conversion with dining room and galley located on upper deck. Seating for 21 passengers on lower deck; (4) 30 passengers on one deck; (5) Accommodation for 22 day and 16 sleeper passengers; (6) Radar equipped for DNL and accommodation for 37 passengers; (7) 30 passengers on one deck; (Islander) Sunderland Mk V (Modified) for Ansett.

G-AGKX, originally Sunderland Mk III ML788, following its conversion to Sandringham I *Himalaya* for BOAC. (Via Martyn Chorlton)

SOLENT 2, 3 AND 4

FIRST FLOWN: 11 November 1946

POWERPLANT: (2 and 3) Four Bristol Hercules 637; (4) Four Bristol Hercules 733

DIMENSIONS (all marks): Span: 112ft 9in; Length: 87ft 8in; Height (fin-top): 34ft 3¼in; Wing area: 1,487sq ft

WEIGHT: Max (AUW): (2) 78,000lb, (3) 78,600lb, (4) 81,000lb

PERFORMANCE: Max speed: (2) 273mph, (3) 267mph, (4) 282mph; Ceiling: (2) 17,000ft, (3) 25,500ft, (4) 17,100ft; Range: (2) 1,800 miles, (3) 2,190 miles, (4) 3,000 miles

PASSENGERS: (2) 34 passengers, (3) 30 passengers, (4) 44 passengers

Solent 3 G-ANAJ *City of Funchal* serving with Aquila Airways, operating from Southampton in May 1954. The ex-Seaford NJ201 was wrecked on 26 September 1956. (*Flight* via Martyn Chorlton)

Even during the post-war period, colour photographs of military aircraft in Britain were rare. This is Mk V SZ565 pictured at Pembroke Dock in the spring of 1950. The flying boat's tour with 201 Squadron only lasted from 10 March to 9 December 1950 and, following a move to 235 OCU at Calshot, the Sunderland crashed and sank on 16 November 1951. After touching down off Calshot, the aircraft rose back into the air for a few seconds and then crashed heavily into the sea. Within seconds, the Sunderland had sunk to the level of the wings, trapping both pilots in the cockpit. Three other crew on board managed to escape but the pilot, Fg Off F. G. Everrett, and co-pilot, Sgt W. Crockart, were drowned. (*Aeroplane*)

Chapter 15

Loyal and Lengthy Service

Royal Air Force (1938–58)

88 (Hong Kong) Squadron, 'En garde' ('Be on your guard')
Reformed 1430 Flight; renumbered at Kai Tak 1 September 1946; DB at Seletar 1 October 1954

Aircraft: GR.5, September 1946 to October 1954: DP199, EJ155, ML745, ML772, ML882, NJ176, NJ272, PP114, PP148, PP155, RN277, RN282, RN291, RN293, RN302, SZ566, SZ570, SZ571, SZ572, SZ577, SZ578, SZ599, VB880, VB883, VB887, VB888

Stations: Kai Tak, Seletar

Dets: Iwakuni, Kai Tak and Seletar

95 Squadron, 'Trans mare exivi' ('I went out over the sea')
Reformed at Pembroke Dock, nucleus from 210 Squadron on 16 January 1941; first operations from Freetown 24 March 1941; flying ceased 25 May 1945; DB at Bathurst/Half Die 30 June 1945

Aircraft: Mk I, January 1941 to December 1942 and March 1943 to November 1943: L5802, L5803 (x2), L5805, N9024, N9027, N9050 (x2), P9623, T9040 (x2), T9041, T9046, T9073, T9074, T9078; Mk II, November 1942 to November 1943: W6062, W6063; Mk III, July 1942 to June 1945: W6015, W6016, W6065, W6076, DP186, DP194, DV956 (x2), DV957, DV963, DV964, DV973, DV974, DW105, DW107, EJ144, EJ163, EJ169, EK587, JM670, JM671, JM677, ML837, ML847

Codes: SE, January 1941 to August 1942; DQ, August 1942 to 1945

Stations: Pembroke Dock, Freetown (Fourah Bay), Jui, Bathurst/Half Die; dets Apapa, Bathurst, Libreville, Pointe Noire, Gibraltar, Fishermans Lake, Dakar and Port Etienne

Sunderland Mk I 'F' of 95 Squadron with both inner engines being test-run at Pembroke Dock prior to departing to Freetown in March 1941. (Via Owen Cooper)

119 Squadron, 'By night and day'
Re-established at Loch Erne 16 April 1942; DB at Pembroke Dock 17 April 1943

Aircraft: Mk II, September 1942 to 1943: W6001, W6002; Mk III, September 1942 to April 1943: W4024, W4028, W4030, DP176, DP179, DV958, DV962, DV971, DV972, EJ133, EJ138, EJ142, JM676

Code: NH, September 1942 to April 1943

Stations: Loch Erne, Pembroke Dock

201 Squadron, 'Hic et ubique' ('Here and everywhere')
Reformed at Calshot, 480 Flight renumbered with Southampton II, 29 January 1929; first Sunderlands, Mk Is N6138 and P9606 received 13 April 1940; DB at Pembroke Dock 28 February 1957

Aircraft: Mk I, April 1940 to January 1942: L2168, L5798, L5800, L5802, L5805, N6133, N6138, N9021, N9049, P9606, P9621, P9622, T9041 (x2), T9046, T9074, T9076, T9077; Mk II, May 1941 to March 1944: T9083, T9084, T9087, W3977, W3978, W3980, W3981, W3982, W6051, W6055, W6059; Mk III, January 1942 to June 1945: W6005, W6010, W6014, DD828, DD829, DD835, DD848, DD855, DD857, DD858, DP185, DP193, DP196, EJ137, EJ150, EJ151, EK579, EK590, EK594, EK595, JM666, ML739, ML742, ML743, ML749, ML759, ML760, ML764, ML768, ML769, ML772, ML782, ML783 (x2), ML784, ML813, ML814, ML817, ML824, ML875, ML876, ML881, ML882, NJ190, NJ194; Mk V,

February 1945 to February 1957: DP198, NJ192, NJ193, NJ264, NJ267 (x2), NJ268, PP112, PP113, PP114, PP115 (x2), PP117 (x2), PP118, PP119, PP120, PP121, PP122, PP144, PP162, PP163, PP164, RN266, RN269, RN270, RN271, RN272, RN273, RN277, RN278, RN282, RN284 (x2), RN285, RN288, RN299, RN300, RN304, SZ565, SZ567, SZ571 (x2), SZ574, SZ575, SZ576, SZ578, SZ598; GR.5: ML778, VB881, VB889

Codes: ZM, September 1939 to August 1943; NS, July 1944 to April 1951; A, April 1951 to February 1957; 201, 1951 to February 1957

Stations: Invergordon, Sullom Voe, Lough Erne, Pembroke Dock, Castle Archdale, Calshot

Dets: Finkenwerder for BAL

Honours: Channel and North Sea, 1939–45; Norway 1940; Atlantic, 1941–45; Bismarck; Biscay, 1941 and 1945; Normandy 1944

202 Squadron, 'Semper vigilate' ('Be always vigilant')
Reformed at Kalafrana, 481 Flight renumbered with Fairey IIID, 29 January 1929; first two Sunderland Mk Is, N6135 and N9021 received April 1939 for conversion training but transferred to 228 Squadron May 1939; last operational sortie 20 September 1942; converted to Catalinas; DB at Castle Archdale 4 June 1945

Aircraft: Mk I, December 1941 to September 1942: N6133, N6135, N9021, N9027, N9050, T9040; Mk II, December 1941 to September 1942: T9084, W3981, W3989 (x2), W3990, W3994, W6002,

A three-ship farewell as 201 Squadron Sunderland Mk Vs leave Castle Archdale for the last time in August 1945. (Via Martyn Chorlton)

Mk V DP198, only recently arrived on 201 Squadron, is moored on the River Thames during Battle of Britain Week, 1956. (*Aeroplane*)

W6003; Mk III, March 1942 to September 1942: W4004, W4024, W4028, W4029, W4030, W4037, DV958, DV962

Codes: TQ, September 1939 to August 1943; AX, May 1941 to August 1943

Stations: Gibraltar, Castle Archdale

Honours: Atlantic, 1939–45; Mediterranean 1940–43; North Africa, 1942–44; Biscay, 1942–44

204 Squadron, 'Praedam mari quaero' ('I seek my prey in the sea')
Reformed at Mount Batten, 481 Flight renumbered with Southampton II, 1 January 1929; first Sunderland Mk I N9028 received 8 June 1939; six aircraft on strength by 2 September 1939; first operational sortie 4 September 1939 by Mk I L5799; DB at Jui 30 June 1945

Aircraft: Mk I, June 1939 to September 1943: L2158, L5798, L5799, L5800, L5802, L5803, N9021, N9022, N9023, N9024 (x2), N9028, N9030, N9044, N9045, N9046, N9047, P9620, T9040, T9041 (x2), T9045, T9048, T9049, T9070, T9072, T9074 (x2); Mk II, June 1941 to March 1943: W3978, W3980, W3981, W6063; Mk III, October 1942 to June 1945: W6012, W6015, W6079, DD833, DD834, DP182, DP188, DV959, DV965, DV966, DV974 (x2), DV991, DW104, EJ145, EK580, EK582, JM669, JM672, JM674, JM680, JM682, JM687, JM710, ML854, ML862

Sunderland Mk I N9030 on the River Medway just days before it was delivered to 204 Squadron on 4 July 1939. Sadly, the flying boat crashed on landing at Mount Batten in poor visibility on 15 October 1939 after returning from a patrol. Four of the six crew on board were killed. (*Aeroplane*)

Mk I T9041 joined 204 Squadron in June 1941, but almost one year to the day, all four engines failed, and the flying boat had to ditch into the sea. Two were killed in the crash, while the remainder spent two uncomfortable days at sea before they were rescued. (Via Owen Cooper)

Codes: RF, April 1939 to September 1939; KG, September 1943 to 1943

Stations: Mount Batten, Sullom Voe, Reykjavik, Gibraltar, Bathurst/Half Die, Jui, Half Die

Dets: Pembroke Dock, Gibraltar, Jui, Port Etienne, Half Dai, Fishermans Lake, Abidjan

Honours: Atlantic, 1940–45; Norway 1940; Arctic 1941

205 Squadron, 'Pertama di Malaya' ('First in Malaya')
Reformed at Koggala with Catalina I, 23 July 1942; operated Sunderlands from March 1945 to
1 January 1955, when merged to form 205/209 Squadron; DB at Changi 31 October 1971

Aircraft: Mk III, 1945: EJ141, ML745, ML797; Mk V/GR.5, June 1945 to May 1959: DP198 (x2), EJ155,
JM667, NJ191, NJ193, NJ268, NJ270, NJ271, NJ272 (x2), NJ274, PP107, PP123, PP124, PP127, PP128, PP129,
PP137, PP144, PP148, PP154, RN269, RN270, RN273, RN278, RN280, RN282, RN288, RN290, RN293 (x2),
RN294, RN300 (x2), RN301, RN303, RN306, SZ560, SZ566 (x2), SZ569, SZ572, SZ577, SZ578 (x2)

Codes: FV; KM

Stations: Koggala, Seletar, Changi; dets Iwakuni, China Bay, Kai Tak, Changi, Seletar

Mk III NJ193 did not arrive on strength with 205 Squadron until June 1953 and was destined to only remain until
January 1955. The flying boat saw out its days with 205/209 Squadron before being SOC at Seletar on 28 February 1957.
(Via Owen Cooper)

205/209 Squadron
Formed from 205 and 209 Squadron on 1 January 1955; Sunderlands withdrawn 1 March 1958 to form 209 Squadron Detachment, which DB 31 May 1958

Aircraft: Mk V, 1955 to 1958: DP198, ML797, PP137

Station: Seletar

209 Squadron, 'Might and Main'
Reformed at Mount Batten with Iris III, 15 January 1930; had a few Sunderlands on strength during 1944; all-Sunderland unit February 1945; merged with 205 Squadron at Seletar 1 January 1955

Aircraft: Mk I, May/June 1938: L2160; Mk V, February 1945 to January 1955: DP198, JM667, NJ177, NJ191, NJ254, NJ260, NJ261, NJ265, NJ273, NJ275, NJ276, PP103, PP105, PP106, PP107, PP108, PP112, PP114, PP130, PP132, PP148, PP150, PP151, PP152, PP154, PP159, PP164, RN264, RN265, RN266, RN277, RN282, RN288, RN293 (x2), RN298, RN300, RN302, RN303, SZ559, SZ560, SZ561, SZ562, SZ565, SZ566, SZ571, SZ573, SZ577, SZ578, SZ599 (x2); GR.5: ML881, ML882, VB882, VB884, VB888

Code: WQ, June 1945 to April 1951

Stations: Kipevu, Koggala, Kai Tak, Seletar; dets Iwakuni, Kai Tak

An unknown Sunderland Mk V of 209 Squadron operating out of Koggala in August 1945. (Via Owen Cooper)

210 Squadron, 'Yn y nwfre yn hedfan' ('Hovering in the heavens')
Reformed at Felixstowe with Southampton II, 1 May 1931; first squadron to receive Sunderlands; Mk I
L2161 first received on 3 July 1938; six on strength by September 1939; DB at Hamworthy Junction
(Poole Harbour) 31 December 1943

Aircraft: Mk I, June 1938 to April 1941: L2161, L2162, L2163, L2164, L2165, L2166, L2167, L2168,
L5798, L5799, L5800, L5802, L5806, L5807, N6135, N9022 (x2), N9024 (x2), N9025, N9026, N9027,
N9047, N9048, N9050, P9600, P9602, P9623, P9624, T9041, T9043, T9044, T9073, T9075, T9076

Codes: VG, May 1939 to September 1939; DA, September 1939 to December 1943

Stations: Pembroke Dock, Tayport, Invergordon, Oban

Dets: Sullom Voe, Reykjavik, Stranraer

Honours: Atlantic, 1939–45

Mk I L2165 'B' at Pembroke Dock in late 1938. The Sunderland was destined to carry out the first Sunderland
operation of World War Two, only to be lost on 17 September 1939. The aircraft failed to find Pembroke Dock after
returning from an anti-submarine patrol at night. After running out of fuel, the Sunderland crashed in the entrance
to Milford Haven in Dale Roads, killing all ten crew on board. (*Aeroplane*)

228 Squadron, 'Auxilium a caelo' ('Help from the sky')
Reformed at Pembroke Dock with Scapa and London I, 15 December 1936; first Sunderland Mk I L5805 received 24 November 1938; DB at Pembroke Dock 4 June 1945

Aircraft: Mk I, November 1938 to August 1941 and November 1941 to March 1943: L2160, L2163, L2168, L5803, L5805, L5806, L5807, N6133, N6135 (x2), N6138, N9020, N9023, N9025 (x2), N9027, N9029, P9600, P9621, P9622, T9046, T9048, T9077; Mk II, November 1941 to March 1943: T9084, T9085, T9086, T9088, T9089, T9109, T9112 (x2), W6004; Mk III, March 1942 to April 1945: W4017, W4026, W4032, DD830, DD834, DD835 [x3], DD836, DD837, DD838, DD847, DD864, DV958, DV967, DV970, DV977, DV978, DV980, DV988, DW110, DW111, EJ139, EJ151, EK572, EK575, JM678 (x2), JM679, JM685, JM708, JM709, JM720, ML745, ML749, ML762, ML763, ML766, ML767, ML769, ML770, ML774, ML782,

Mk V PP118 about to take off from Pembroke Dock in 1945 whilst serving with 228 Squadron. (*Aeroplane*)

ML812, ML815, ML877, ML878, ML879, ML880, NJ171, NJ191, NJ192, PP136; Mk V, February 1945 to June 1945: ML796, PP117, PP118, PP120, PP121, PP144, PP163, PP164, RN277, RN278, RN283, RN285

Codes: TO, April 1939 to May 1939; BH, May 1939 to September 1939; DQ, September 1939 to August 1943; NM, 1943; UE, July 1944 to June 1945

Stations: Pembroke Dock, Alexandria, Aboukir, Kalafrana, Bathurst, Stranraer, Oban, Lough Erne/ Castle Archdale; dets Kalafrana, Alexandria, Calshot

230 Squadron, 'Kita chari jauh' ('We seek far')
Reformed at Pembroke Dock with Singapore III, 1 December 1934; first Sunderland Mk I L2159 received 25 June 1938; eight on strength by January 1939; flew 1,000 sorties in Berlin Airlift; DB at Pembroke Dock 28 February 1957

Aircraft: Mk I, June 1938 to January 1943: L2159, L2160, L2161, L2163, L2164, L2166, L5801, L5803, L5804, L5806, N9029, N9030, T9050, T9071; Mk II, October 1941 to September 1942: W3987; Mk III, March 1942 to April 1945: W4021, W4022, W4023, DP180, DP189, EJ131, EJ132, EJ135, EJ136, EJ140, EJ141, EJ143, EJ155, JM673, JM711, ML797, ML800, ML817, ML846, ML861, ML865, ML868; Mk V, February 1945 to February 1957: DP200, EJ153, JM718 (x2), ML796, NJ264, NJ277, PP107, PP115 (x2), PP117, PP118, PP122, PP115 (x2), PP117, PP118, PP122, PP145, PP146, PP147, PP149, PP152, PP155 (x2), PP157, PP158, PP161, PP164, RN268, RN269, RN270, RN278, RN290, RN299, RN303 (x2), RN304, SZ560, SZ567 (x2), SZ572, SZ572, SZ575, SZ577, SZ581, SZ582; GR.5: ML763, VB882, VB887

Codes: FV, April 1939 to September 1939; NM, September 1939 to January 1943; DX, 1942 to December 1942; 4X; B, April 1951 to 1956; 230, 1956 to February 1957

Stations: Seletar, Koggala, Alexandria, Aboukir, Fanara, Dar-es-Salaam, Akyab, Rangoon, Red Hills Lake, Pembroke Dock, Castle Archdale, Calshot; Dets: Trincomalee, Colombo, Penang, Koggala, Kalafrana, Aboukir, Scaramanga, Bizerta, Jui, Tulear, Pamanzi, Diego Garcia, Addu Atoll, Kelai, Lake Indawgyi, Red Hills Lake, Seletar, Finkenwerder (BAL)

Honours: Mediterranean, 1940–43; Egypt and Libya, 1940–43; Greece, 1940–41; Malta, 1940–42; Eastern Waters, 1943–45; North Burma, 1944; Burma, 1945

240 Squadron, 'Sjo-Vordur Lopt-Vordur' ('Guardian of the sea, guardian of the sky')
Reformed at Red Hills Lake (212 retitled) with Catalina I, IV and Sunderland V, 1 July 1945 from elements of 212 and 240 Squadrons; DB at Koggala 21 March 1946

Aircraft: Mk V, July 1945 to March 1946: NJ272, NJ273, NJ275, NJ276, PP126, PP130, PP131, RN291, RN292, RN297, RN298, SZ564

Code: BN, 1945 to 1946

Stations: Red Hills Lake, Koggal; Dets: Bally, China Bay, Penang, Rangoon

Mk V ML817 served with 230 Squadron from January 1955 to February 1957, when it was transferred to the FBSU at Calshot and SOC in October. (Via Owen Cooper)

Mk V PP130 being manhandled towards the slipway at Red Hills Lake, Madras, India, in July 1945. The Sunderland served with 240 Squadron from July 1945 to March 1951. (*Aeroplane*)

246 Squadron
Reformed at Bowmore with Sunderland Mk III, 5 August 1942; declared operational 12 December 1942; first operational sortie 12 December 1942; DB at Bowmore 30 April 1943

Aircraft: Mk II, 1942 to April 1943: W6056, W6057, W6058, W6060; Mk III, October 1942 to April 1943: W6066, DD845, DD846, DV978, DV979, DV980, EJ137, EJ139

Codes: OY, August 42 to April 43; VU, August 42 to April 43

Station: Bowmore

259 Squadron, 'Haya ingia napigane' ('Get in a fight')
Reformed at Kipevu with Catalina IB, 16 February 1943; aircraft transferred to SAAF; DB at Dar-es-Salaam 1 May 1945

Aircraft: Mk III, February 1943 to 1945; Mk V, March 1945 to April 1945

Station: Dar-es-Salaam

270 Squadron, 'Petamus' ('Let us ask')
Reformed at Jui with Catalina IB, 12 November 1942; Sunderlands from 5 December 1943; DB at Apapa 30 June 1945

Aircraft: Mk III, December 1943 to June 1945: DP190, DW106, DW108, DW109, DW111, EJ164, EK584, EK585, EK588, EK589, EK592, EK593, ML844, ML849, ML853, ML857, ML867, ML874

Station: Apapa

Mk III DW109 served exclusively with 270 Squadron during the unit's 19-month existence, before going into store with 57 MU at Wig Bay, only to be scrapped in 1947. (Via Owen Cooper)

Royal Australian Air Force (1939–46)

10 Squadron, 'Strike First'
Formed at Point Cook on 1 July 1939; first Sunderland Mk I N9048 received 11 September 1939; squadron declared operational 1 February 1940; first operational sortie 6 February 1940 by Mk I P9605; last wartime sortie 7 May 1945 by Mk III NJ256; squadron ceased operations on 1 June 1945; DB Mount Batten October 1945; total war operational sorties 3,239; personnel fatalities 151.

Aircraft: Mk I, September 1939 to 1943: L2163, N9047, N9048, N9049 (x2), N9050, P9600, P9601, P9602, P9603, P9604, P9605, P9606, T9047, T9071, T9072, T9075; Mk II, 1941 to 1943: W3979, W3983 (x2), W3984, W3985, W3986 (x2), W3993, W3994 (x2), W3997; Mk III, November 1943 to 1945: W3999, W4003, W4004 (x2), W4019, W4020, W4024, W4030, DD852, DD865, DD867, DP177, DP179, DP192, DV958, DV969, DV993, DW113, EK573, EK574, EK575, EK586, EK594, JM678, JM684, JM685, JM721, ML813, ML822, ML828, ML829, ML830, ML831, ML839, ML848, ML856, NJ253, NJ254, NJ255, NJ256, PP135, PP138, PP139, PP142; Mk V, 1944 to 1945: NJ193, NJ264, NJ267, NJ268, PP113, PP114, PP115, PP119, PP122, PP162, RN282, RN300

Code: RB, September 1939 to June 1945

Stations: Pembroke Dock, Mount Batten, Oban, Kalafrana

Honours: Atlantic, 1939–45; Biscay, 1940–45; Mediterranean, 1940–43; Biscay Ports, 1940–45; English Channel and North Sea, 1939–45; Bismarck; Normandy, 1944

The sheer scale of the Sunderland is shown to good effect while groundcrew work on Sunderland Mk I P9603 of 10 Squadron RAAF at Pembroke Dock. On 1 July 1940, in the hands of Flt Lt Gibson, P9603 shared the sinking of U-26. (Via Martyn Chorlton)

The 11 crew of a 10 Squadron RAAF Sunderland walk up the slip at Mount Batten in 1945. (Via Owen Cooper)

40 Squadron
Formed at Townsville, Queensland, with six Sunderlands ferried out from the UK on 31 March 1944; first two left UK on 27 January 1944 and the rest on 1 March 1944; to Port Moresby, New Guinea, 22 July 1944; to New South Wales March 1946; DB 19 June 1946

Aircraft: Mk III, March 1944 to June 1946

Codes: A, 26-4 (ex-ML733)

Stations: Townsville, Port Moresby

461 Squadron, 'They shall not pass unseen'
Formed at Mount Batten with Sunderland II, 26 April 1942; first operational sortie 1 July 1942; last operational sortie 18 June 1945; DB at Pembroke Dock 4 June 1945; returned to Australia 31 October 1945; casualties: 86 killed in 14 aircraft.

Aircraft: Mk I, April 1942 to May 1943: L5802; Mk II, April 1942 to May 1943: T9085, T9088, T9090, T9109, T9111, T9113, T9114, T9115; Mk III, August 1942 to June 1945: DD853, DD866, DP196, DP199, DP200, DV960, DV961, DV962, DV968, DV985, DV986, DV989, EJ132, EJ133, EJ134, EJ138, EJ142, EJ153, EJ154, EK575, EK577, EK578, EK590, JM675, JM676, JM678, JM683, JM685, JM686, JM707, ML735, ML739, ML740, ML741, ML743, ML744, ML746, ML747, ML748, ML757, ML758, ML771, ML774, ML778, ML781, ML827, ML831, ML879; Mk V, February 1945 to June 1945: NJ193, NJ264, NJ267, NJ268, PP113, PP114, PP115, PP116, PP119, PP122, PP162, RN279, RN280, RN282

Code: UT, April 1942 to August 1943 and July 1944 to June 1945

Stations: Mount Batten, Hamworthy, Pembroke Dock

Left: 40 Squadron RAAF first commanding officer was Wg Cdr Vic Hodgkinson DFC, MID, MRAeS. (Via Owen Cooper)

Below: Possibly taken not long before the unit disbanded in June 1945, the whole of 461 Squadron pose for the last time with one of their Sunderland Mk Vs. (Via Owen Cooper)

To RAAF
Aircraft: Mk III: ML730, ML731, ML732, ML733, ML734

Royal Canadian Air Force (1942–45)

422 (Flying Yachtsman) Squadron, 'The arm shall do it'
Formed at Lough Erne with Lerwick I, 2 April 1942; first Sunderland received 1 November 1942; first operation flown by Mk III W6026; last operational sorties by five aircraft flown on 1–2 June 1945; casualties: 42 killed in nine aircraft on operations; 1,116 operational sorties; DB at Bassingbourn 4 September 1945

Aircraft: Mk III, November 1942 to June 1945: W6026, W6027, W6028, W6029, W6030, W6031, W6032, W6033, W6066, DD831, DD838, DD845, DD846, DD850, DD854, DD855, DD861, DP178, DV970, DV988, DV990, DV994, EJ151, EK576, EK591, EK594, EK595, JM679, JM712, ML744, ML750, ML758, ML759, ML769, ML773, ML777, ML778, ML781, ML814, ML816, ML821, ML836, ML879, ML883, ML884, NJ170, NJ172, NJ173, NJ174, NJ175, NJ176, NJ189

Codes: 2, August 1943 to July 1944; DG, July 1944 to September 1945; YI, 1945

Stations: Oban, Bowmore, St Angelo, Castle Archdale, Pembroke Dock; dets: Jui

Honours: Atlantic, 1942–45; English Channel and North Sea 1944–45; Normandy, 1944; Biscay, 1944–45

422 Squadron Mk III 'P' building up speed on Lough Erne in February 1944. (Via Owen Cooper)

423 (Bald Eagle) Squadron, 'Quaerimus et petimus' ('We search and strike')
Formed at Oban with Sunderland II, 18 May 1942; first Sunderland Mk II W6001 received 17 July 1942; first sortie 23 August 1942 by Mk II W6053; last operational sortie 31 May 1945 by Mk III ML777; casualties: 40 killed in six aircraft on operations; 1,392 operational sorties; DB at Bassingbourn 4 September 1945

Aircraft: Mk II, July 1942 to April 1943: W6000, W6001, W6052, W6053, W6061, W6064; Mk III, September 1942 to May 1945: W6006 (x2), W6007, W6008, W6009, W6011, W6013, W6068, DD828, DD838, DD843, DD849, DD853, DD858, DD859, DD860, DD862, DD863, DD867, DP181, DP191, DP193, DP198, DV978, DV980, DW111, DW112, EJ156, EJ157, EJ158, EK575, EK581, EK583, JM666, JM667, ML746, ML777, ML783, ML784, ML817, ML823, ML825, ML883, NJ182, NJ183, NJ184, NJ185, NJ186, NJ187

Code: AB, May 1942 to August 1943; 3, August 1943 to July 1944 and 1944 to May 1945

Stations: Oban, Lough Erne/Castle Archdale

Honours: Atlantic, 1942–45; English Channel and North Sea 1944–45; Normandy, 1944; Biscay, 1944

EK583, a Sunderland Mk III belonging to 423 Squadron, is pictured on Castle Archdale's large apron and slipway in early 1944. (*Aeroplane*)

France (Aeronavale) (1943–62)

343 (Free French) Squadron

First Sunderlands arrived July 1943 to equip French 3E and 4E (Flotille 1); merged October 1943 to form Flotille 7F; retitled 343 Squadron RAF at Dakar from Flotille 7F with Sunderland Mk III, 29 November 1943; DB at Dakar 27 November 1945 and transferred to French control

Aircraft: Mk III, November 1943 to November 1945: W6080, DP182, DP187, DV965, DV985, DV986, DV987, EJ163, EJ168, JM688, JM689, JM704, JM706, ML841, ML851, ML854, ML870, ML871

Stations: Dakar; Port Etienne

Aeronavale: Following 343 Squadron's disbandment, the Aeronavale acquired four batches of Sunderlands during the post-1945 period. These were ML750, NJ172 received in 1947 followed by a batch of 14 aircraft made up of: ML757, ML764, ML778, ML779, ML781, ML796, ML799, ML816, ML819, ML820, ML821, ML866, ML872 and NJ170. Four additional Sunderlands arrived in 1952, which were ML739, ML877, NJ182 and NJ190 and, finally, in 1957, ML800, ML824, RN284, SZ571 and SZ576. By 1960, the flying boats began to be run down and, by 30 January 1962, ML796 and RN284 became the last Sunderlands to serve with the Aeronavale.

Units included: 4th GR Squadron, Flotille 1FE, Flotille 7F; (Mk V ML824), Flotille 7FE; (Mk III JM705, JM706; Mk V ML796), Flotille 27F; (Mk V ML824), Escadrilles 12S; (Mk V ML824), Escadrilles 50S; (Mk V ML824), Escadrilles 53S

Mk V NJ190 was delivered to the Aeronavale on 19 February 1952, going on to serve with Flotille 27F, Escadrille 50S and Escadrille 53S before being SOC on 23 August 1960. (*Aeroplane*)

Portuguese Navy (1941)

On 13 February 1941, Sqn Ldr Lombard, Flt Lt Evison, Fg Off Bowie, Sgt Banfield and seven other unnamed aircrew were tasked with ferrying 95 Squadron Sunderland Mk I P9623 from Mount Batten to Gibraltar. The aircraft, 'SE-E' *The Lazy E* took off at 2345hrs, but, by the early hours of the following morning, was running low on fuel because of a strong headwind that had not been forecasted. It was also still over 250 miles short of its destination. Sqn Ldr Lombard had no choice but to alight near Setubal in Portugal, where the crew and aircraft were inevitably interned within the neutral country.

The Sunderland was briefly taken on charge by the Portuguese Navy, complete with national markings, although the registration, if any, is unknown. It is not clear how many times the aircraft was

Right and opposite: Caramujo,
Portugal. Tel. Almada 125.
(Leslie H Howard, *Flight* via *Aeroplane*)

flown by the Portuguese, but, against popular belief the photographic evidence supplied shows P9623 flying at least once over Lisbon. The Sunderland was officially SOC by the RAF on 20 May 1941 (but this does not mean that the Portuguese did not fly it beyond this date). It was flown several times, but the lack of proper maintenance support and spare parts saw the engines suffer and the inevitable failure occurred, coupled with the loss of a propeller on its last flight.

With regard to the crew, they all managed to 'escape' with the help of two locals and the Royal Navy on 23 March 1941. The 'locals' were a businessman from Aveiro and a Portuguese Air Force colonel who actually knew Sqn Ldr Lombard, having been on the same RAF course before the war broke out. The Portuguese government was not interested in RAF aircrew, making the task of getting the airmen home easier. Both of the men who helped the crew were given medals after the war for helping many more RAF airmen to get home through the war.

Royal New Zealand Air Force (1943–67)
5 Squadron, 'Keitou Kalawaca Na Wasaliwa' ('We span the ocean')
Hobsonville in 1967; currently extant with P-3 Orions.

Aircraft: MR.5, 1953 to 1967: NZ4105, NZ4108, NZ4109, NZ4110, NZ4111, NZ4112, NZ4114, NZ4115, NZ4116, NZ4117, NZ4120

Code: KN, 1953 to 1967

Stations: Lauthala Bay, Whenuapai

6 Squadron, 'Vigilance and patience'
Reformed at Hobsonville as 6 (Marchitime) Squadron in April 1952 with Catalinas and Sunderlands; DB in August 1957

Aircraft: Mk III, May 1952 to November 1953: NZ1404; MR.5, 1952 to August 1957: NZ4106, NZ4113, NZ4118, NZ4119, NZ4120

Code: XX, 1952 to 1957

Station: Hobsonville

490 Squadron, 'Taniwha kei runga' ('The Taniwha is in the air')
Formed at Jui with Catalina IB, 28 March 1943; Sunderlands from 4 May 1944 to 1 August 1945; first two Sunderlands arrived at Jui on 4 May 1944, Mk III ML850 and ML852; first Sunderland operational sortie 17 May 1944 by Mk III ML850; DB at Jui on 30 June 1945

Aircraft: Mk III, May 1944 to June 1945: EJ135, EJ165, EJ169, ML810, ML835, ML850, ML852, ML857, ML859, ML862, ML863, ML864, ML869; Mk V, 1944 to June 1945: JM717

Code: P6, July 1944 to August 1945

Stations: Jui

Dets: Stranraer, Fishermans Lake, Apapa, Adidjan, Bathhurst/Half Dia

MOTU and MRSU (Maritime Operational Training Unit and Maritime Reconnaissance and Support Unit) Operated several Sunderland MR.5s from Hobsonville during 1956

Aircraft: MR.5: NZ4108, NZ4113, NZ4114, NZ4118, NZ4119

Royal Norwegian Air Force (1943–45)

330 (Norwegian) Squadron, 'Trygg havet' ('Guarding the seas')
Reformed at Reykjavik with N3P-B, 25 April 1941; first Sunderland Mk I W6064 received 9 February 1943; DB at Stavanger/ Sola 21 November 1945 and transferred to Norwegian control

Aircraft: Mk II, March 1943 to March 1944: T9083, T9112, W6052, W6053, W6059, W6061, W6064; Mk III, February 1943 to April 1945: W6027, W6030, W6067, W6068, W6075, DD835, DD843, DD844, DD851, DD856, DP178, DP181, DP183, DP184, EJ137, EJ138, JM666, JM667, ML758, ML780, ML817, ML818, ML819, ML824, NJ177, NJ178, NJ179, NJ180, NJ180, NJ188, NJ190, PP140; Mk V, April 1945 to November 1945: ML814, ML827, ML878, NJ170, NJ172, RN267

Codes: GS, May 1941 to March 1943; WH, 1944 to November 1945

Stations: Oban, Sullom Voe, Stavanger/Sola

Dets: Reykjavik, Budayeri

South African Air Force (1945–55)

35 Squadron, 'Shaya Amanzi' ('Strike the Water')
Formed at Congella 15 February 1945 from 262 Squadron (RAF) with Catalinas; first three
Sunderlands received 24 April 1945; last official SAAF Sunderland flight made by GR.5 1710 'RB-D' on
8 October 1957; re-equipped with Shackleton MR.3s during 1954 and 1955

Aircraft: GR.5, April 1945 to October 1956: 1701 (ex-NJ262), 1702 (ex-PP125), 1703 (ex-PP109),
1704 (ex-RN279), 1705 (ex-RN296), 1706 (ex-RN305), 1707 (ex-NJ258), 1708 (ex-NJ263), 1709 (ex-
ML798), 1710 (ex-RN281), 1711 (ex-NJ266), 1712 (ex-PP156), 1713 (ex-NJ259), 1714 (ex-RN295),
1715 (ex-PP104), PP153

Code: RB, from 1945

Stations: Congella Dunbar, Lake Umsingazi

Ex-PP109 Mk V was transferred to 35 Squadron SAAF on 29 May 1945. Named *House Mouse*, the aircraft is
pictured on 13 May 1955, destined to be SOC after an accident on 28 August 1957. (*Aeroplane*)

RAF Second Line and Support Units
(Where known, one representative serial is displayed)

(1) FBSU (Flying Boat Servicing Unit)
Formed 12 March 1942 as the FBSU in 15 Group at Wig Bay; redesignated No. 1 FBSU 25 September 1942; absorbed by 57 MU 1 February 1944

Aircraft: Mk III: DD834; Mk V: JM715

3 FBSU
Formed 25 September 1942 out of the FBSU in 19 Group at Pembroke Dock; DB December 1944

4 FBSU
Formed out of the FBSU in 15 Group at Ganavan Sands/Oban April 1944

4 OTU (Operational Training Unit)
Formed 16 March 1941 in 17 Group at Stranraer to train flying boat crews to operational standard; 15–21 June 1942 to Invergordon, renamed Alness 10 February 1943; December 1941 first Sunderlands arrive; to Pembroke Dock 15 August 1946; to Calshot July 1947 and retitled 235 OCU.

Aircraft: Mk I, December 1941 to 1944: L2160, L2168, L5800, L5802, N6138, N9024, N9044, N9045, N9050, P9600, P9604, P9605, P9606, T9040, T9042, T9049, T9076, T9077; Mk II, December 1941 to 1944: T9083, T9088, T9115, W3980, W3981, W3989, W3990, W3992, W3997, W6001, W6002, W6051, W6056, W6060, W6064; Mk III, 1942 to 1946: W4027, W4028, W4031, W4033, W4034, W4035, W4037, W6005, W6006, W6009, W6010, W6012, W6014, W6015, W6026, W6027, DD828, DD832, DD838, DD839, DD840, DD841, DD842, DD843, DD844, DD850, DD851, DD855, DD856, DP178, DP184, DP185, DP197, DP200, DV961, DV970, DV988, DV992, DV994, DW111, EJ137, EJ142, EJ149, EJ152, EK573, EK576, EK577, EK590, EK591, JM668, JM679, JM683, JM686, JM713, JM718, ML736, ML737, ML738, ML739, MJ749, ML767, ML779, ML796, ML801, ML820, ML826, ML841, NJ190, NJ257, NJ258; Mk V, 1945 to 1946: EJ155, ML739, ML741 (x2), ML747, ML757, ML778, ML780, ML781, ML796, ML812, ML816, ML866, ML873, ML875, ML882, NJ191, NJ192, NJ269, PP111, PP112, PP113, PP137, PP141, PP160, PP161, RN272, RN285, RN286, RN287, SZ568, SZ569, SZ571, SZ575, VB886, VB888,

Codes: TA, to July 1947

Stations: Invergordon, Pembroke Dock

5 FBSU
Formed 25 September 1942 in 17 Group at Invergordon (Dalmore); DB December 1944

6 FBSU
Formed 13 September 1943 from the FBRS in 16 Group at Calshot; DB August 1945

7 FE (Far East)
Details unknown; Mk III, DD835

DP200, a Mk V, had a busy service career that stretched from March 1944 until October 1956. The Sunderland is pictured at Invergordon, serving with 4 OTU in late 1945. (Via Martyn Chorlton)

11 FBFU (Flying Boat Fitting Unit)
Formed 15 May 1943 in 15 Group at Wig Bay; absorbed by 57 MU 8 October 1943

12 FBFU
Proposed to form July 1943 at Pembroke Dock

57 MU (Maintenance Unit)
Formed 8 October 1943 absorbing 11 FBSU in 43 Group at Wig Bay; absorbed 1 FBSU 1 February 1944; DB 1 October 1951 and taken over by Short & Harland

Aircraft: Mk III, October 1943 to 1951 (Representative): DD834; Mk V, 1944 to 1951: JM715, ML796, NJ268, PP121, PP123, SZ599, TX293

131 OTU
Formed at Killadeas 20 July 1942 in 15 Group to train flying boat crews on the Catalina; Sunderlands introduced from May 1944 onwards using satellites at Boa Island; 19 Sunderland on strength by July 1944; Sunderland commitment transferred to 4 OTU 13 February 1945

Aircraft: Mk II, May 1944 to June 1945: W6056; Mk III, May 1944 to June 1945: W6007, W6011, W6032, W6066, W6068, DD829, DD835 (x2), DD843, DD845, DD847, DD849, DD853, DD854, DD867, DP191, DP193, DV960, DV978, DV980, DV989, EK579, EK583, JM666, ML808, ML836, ML842

The ultimate Belfast-produced Sunderland was Mk V SZ599, pictured here on an air test from 57 MU, Wig Bay in 1954. (*Aeroplane*)

Codes: CL, DE and DH

235 OCU (Operational Conversion Unit)
Formed 7 July 1947 at Calshot from 4 OTU to train flying boat crews with an establishment of five Sunderlands; DB into 19 Group 17 October 1953 and all personnel and aircraft transferred to the FBTS at Pembroke Dock

Aircraft: Mk III, 1947: ML817; Mk V, July 1947 to October 1953: EJ153, JM718, NJ265, PP118, PP130, PP141, PP163, RN266, RN272, RN284, RN288, SZ565, SZ568, SZ569, SZ575, SZ576, SZ580; GR.5: ML780, ML815, VB888

Code: TA, July 1947 to October 1953

272 MU
Formed 1 August 1945 as Flying Boat Long Term Storage Unit in 41 Group at Killadeas; DB 28 February 1947

Aircraft: Mk III: W4003, ML736 (Representative)

Above: Sunderland Mk III W6066 of 131 OTU at a very cold Killadeas during the winter of 1944/1945. (Via Martyn Chorlton)

Right: Created from 4 OTU in 1947, 235 OCU existed as a Sunderland training unit at Calshot until 1953. This is Sunderland Mk V SZ568, which was SOC on 19 October 1956. (Via Martyn Chorlton)

302 FTU (Ferry Training Unit)

Formed 30 September 1942 in 15 Group at Lough Erne to train crews to ferry flying boats to overseas units; to Stranraer 1 December 1942; to Oban 21–22 July 1943; absorbed 308 FTU with det at Alness 1 January 1944; to Killadeas 15–28 April 1945; DB 1 April 1946

Aircraft: Mk II, 1942: W3989; Mk III, 1942 to 1946: W4002, W4003, W4017, DD865, DD866, DV956, DW112, EJ135, EJ163, EJ165, EJ168, EJ169, EK593, JM667, JM717, ML792, ML793, ML794, ML795, ML799, ML800, ML801, ML809, ML810, ML811, ML835, ML837, ML841, ML845, ML846, ML847, ML849, ML850, ML851, ML852, ML853, ML854, ML855, ML857, ML858, ML859, ML860, ML861, ML862, ML863, ML864, ML865, ML867, ML868, ML869, ML970, ML871, ML872, EK595, EK596, ML794, ML795, NJ258 (x2); Mk V, 1944 to 1946: EJ171, EJ172, JM714, JM719, JM720, ML739, ML741, ML757, ML812, ML874, ML878, NJ259, NJ260, NJ261, NJ262, NJ263, NJ265, NJ266, NJ270, NJ271, NJ272, NJ273, NJ274, NJ275, NJ276, NJ277, PP103, PP104, PP105, PP106, PP107, PP108, PP109, PP123, PP124, PP125, PP126, PP128, PP129, PP130, PP131, PP132, RN264, RN265, RN266, RN268, RN269, RN279, RN280, RN281, RN287, RN288, RN289, RN290, RN291, RN292, RN293, RN294, RN295, RN296, RN297, RN298, RN299, RN301, RN302, RN303, RN304, RN305, RN306, SZ559, SZ560, SZ561, SZ562, SZ563, SZ564, SZ565, SZ566, SZ567, SZ568, SZ569, SZ570, SZ571, SZ575, VB880, VB882, VB883, VB884, VB885, VB888

308 FTU and TFU (Test Flying Unit)
Formed 22 March 1943 in 19 Group at Pembroke Dock as No. 308 Ferry Training and Test Flying Unit to ferry Sunderlands to overseas units; redesignated 308 FTU 7 May 1943; absorbed by 302 FTU at Oban 12 January 1944

Aircraft: Mk III, 1943 to 1944: W6080, DP187, DV985, DV986, DV987, EJ138, EJ164, JM688, JM689, JM704, JM705, JM706, JM711, ML797

Sunderland Mk V RN288 seen on Lough Erne, Northern Island, in May 1945, during the ten days it served with 302 OTU at Killadeas before being transferred to 205 Squadron. (Via Owen Cooper)

1430 Flt
Reformed 5 August 1945 as 1430 (Flying Boat Transport) in ACSEA with five Sunderland at Kai Tak; redesignated 88 Squadron 1 September 1946

Aircraft: Mk V, August 1945 to September 1946: SZ564

ASWDU (Air-Sea Warfare Development Unit)
Formed 1 January 1945 ex-CCDU at Thorney Island with Sunderland/Flying Boat det at Calshot.

Aircraft: Mk III: ML763, ML785, NJ182; Mk V: PP122

Code: P9

BTU (Bombing Trials Unit)
The BTU was based at West Freugh and was generally composed of land-based aircraft. It is possible that Sunderland RN294 was seconded to the BTU for bombing trials from 205 Squadron.

Aircraft: Mk V: RN294

CCFIS (Coastal Command Flying Instructor's School)
Formed ex-12 FIS (Flying Instructor's School) at St Angelo with a flying boat detachment at Killadeas on 2 February 1945; moved to Turnberry 9 June 1945 with the flying boat detachment moving to Alness, which continued from 16 July–29 October 1945; CCFIS moved to Tain 13 November 1945 and disbanded into the CCIS.

Aircraft: Mk III: ML741 (Representative)

CCIS (Coastal Command Instructor's School)
Formed 29 October 1945 from CCFIS and CCGIS (Coastal Command Ground Instructor's School) and Turnberry with aircraft that included at least two Sunderland Mk Vs; DB 1 April 1946.

Aircraft: Mk V: ML741, ML781, NJ268 (Representative)

Far East
No details on this unit other than the following aircraft credited to it; Mk III: DD865, DD866, ML797, ML799; Mk V; RN289, RN299, RN303, SZ563

FBMU (Flying Boat Modification Unit)
Formed at Caird's Yard, Greenock, mainly tasked with converting Mk IIIs to Mk V standard.

FBRS/B (Flying Boat Repair Station), Kisumu
Formed 1 November 1942 at Kisumu to carry out major servicing and repairs in East Africa; by 31 March 1949, station was in civilian hands.

FBTS (Flying Boat Training Squadron)

Reformed 17 October 1953, ex-235 OCU at Pembroke Dock for similar duties with three Sunderland Vs; DB 5 October 1956, just prior to the last flying boat squadron's disbanding.

Aircraft: Mk V, October 1953 to October 1956: JM718, NJ180, RN303, RN304, RN266, SZ560, SZ571

FBSU
Formed 1 October 1951 in 41 Group at Wig Bay to store Sunderlands on disbandment of 57 MU; civilian operated unit by Short Brothers & Harland Ltd; DB 31 October 1957.

Aircraft: Mk V: SZ584

Iraq CF (Communication Flight)
'B' Flight of the CF operated Sunderlands from Lake Habbaniya until the early 1950s.

Aircraft: Mk III: DW112, EK595, JM711

MAEE (Marine Aircraft Experimental Establishment)
Various marks of Sunderland were trialled by the MAEE while they were operating from Felixstowe and later Helensburgh/Rhu from 1938 and 1 August 1945.

Aircraft: Prototype: K4774; Mk IL: 2158, L2159, N9021, P9604, T9042; Mk II: T9083, W3976, W6050, W6051; Mk III: DD832, DV967, DV976, JM681, JM713, JM714, ML735, ML750, ML765, ML817; Mk V: PP109, PP151, PP162, RN297, SZ599, TX293

The first of many Sunderlands to pass through the MAEE was the prototype K4774, seen here at Felixstowe in 1938. (*Aeroplane*)

Short
Aircraft: (Representative) Mk I: T9042; Mk III: DV576; Mk V: PP151

Station Flight Koggala
Aircraft: Mk III: ML865; Mk V: RN280, RN302

TRE (Telecommunications Research Establishment) (FE)
Aircraft: Mk V: SZ561

The unsung heroes at work on a BOAC Sunderland at Hythe in 1946. Hythe is located ten miles south of Southampton on the western shore of Southampton Water. The hangar in which these engineers are working was erected by May-Harden-May Ltd in 1925 and was first acquired by Supermarine. By 1937, the hangar and expanding site was in the hands of Imperial Airways and then BOAC, which operated its Sunderlands from there until 1950. The US Army carried out small boat repairs at Hythe from 1967 and remarkably only left in 2006. As a result, the original large hangar and several period buildings remain in situ. (*Aeroplane*)

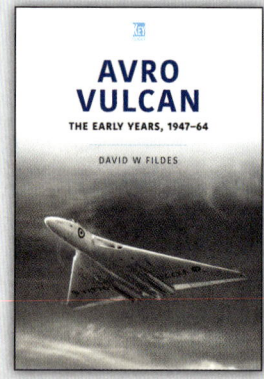
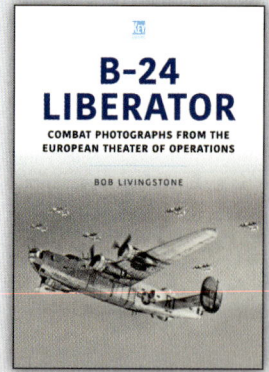

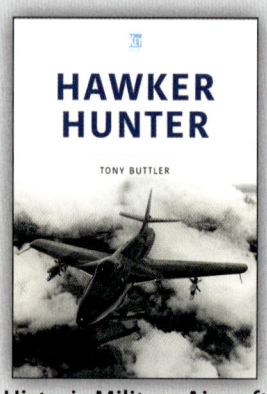
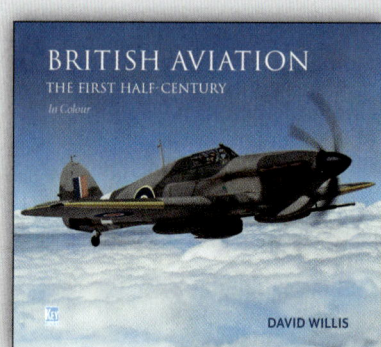
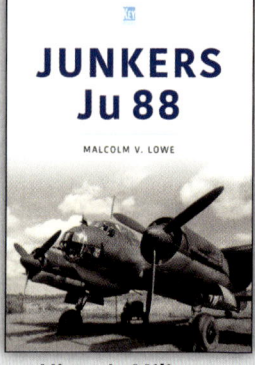